Opening Day and Other Neuroses

Books by WILLIAM G. TAPPLY

Novels
(in order of appearance)

DEATH AT CHARITY'S POINT
THE DUTCH BLUE ERROR
FOLLOW THE SHARKS
THE MARINE CORPSE
DEAD MEAT
A VOID IN HEARTS
THE VULGAR BOATMAN
DEAD WINTER

Nonfiction

THOSE HOURS SPENT OUTDOORS:
REFLECTIONS
ON HUNTING AND FISHING

OPENING DAY
and Other Neuroses

William G. Tapply

L&B Lyons & Burford, Publishers

Printed in the United States of America

10 9 8 7 6 5 4 3 2

Library of Congress Cataloging-in-Publication Data

Tapply, William G.
Opening day and other neuroses / William G. Tapply.
p.   cm.
"Nick Lyons books."
ISBN 1-55821-071-7 : $16.95
1. Fishing. I. Title.
SH441.T37   1990
799.1—dc20   89-48557

CIP

For Andy Gill

—

Not just a fictional character

ACKNOWLEDGMENTS

Many of the pieces in this volume are adapted from previously published material, mostly in *Field & Stream*. In virtually all cases I have been driven by the writer's obsessive need to refine and edit *ad nauseum* in the hope of making things better. As a result, a lot of this stuff will scarcely be recognizable as having evolved from what it originally was. In a few cases I have even changed the titles. In no case am I confident that I have made any real improvement. But I do feel better for having done it.

"Opening Day" originally appeared in the *Field & Stream Fishing* annual of 1988.

"Bait Hunting with Skeeter" appeared in *Field & Stream* (June, 1989) under the title "Skeeter and the Great Bait Debate."

"Trickle Trout" appeared in *New England Game & Fish* (April, 1988) under the title "Trouting the Trickles."

"Toads in the Scumline" appeared in *Field & Stream* (October, 1989).

"Bighorn of Plenty" appeared in *Field & Stream* (January, 1989).

"The Giant Tarpon of Belize" appeared in the *Field & Stream Saltwater Fishing* annual of 1989 under the title "Tarpon on the Fly."

"Beetles at High Noon" appeared in *Field & Stream* (July, 1989) under the title "The All Day Beetle."

"Midge Phobia" appeared in *Field & Stream* (August, 1989) under the title "Midge Magic."

"The Hair of the Deer" (Parts I and II) appeared in *Field & Stream* (November, 1985) under the title "Hair of the Deer."

"A Shad in the Dark" appeared in *Field & Stream* (May, 1988).

"Big Mouths in Small Places" appeared in *Field & Stream* (August, 1988).

Part of "The *Newsweek* Papers" appeared in *Newsweek* (April 10, 1989).

Sections from "A Guy I Know" are from the novels *Dead Winter* (Delacorte, 1989), *Dead Meat* (Charles Scribner's Sons, 1987), and *Follow the Sharks* (Charles Scribner's Sons, 1985).

My thanks to all the worthy editors who have encouraged me along the way—especially Nick Lyons, Duncan Barnes, Betsy Rapoport, Susanne Kirk, and Jackie Farber—and to all the others whose advice, counsel, and support have been deeply appreciated, including Jed Mattes, Andy Gill, Rick Boyer, and, of course, H. G. Tapply.

CONTENTS

INTRODUCTION

For most of my angling life (which is most of my entire life, since I can't recall a time when fishing wasn't important to me) I happily threw whatever kind of line was handy—bait-casting, spinning, fly, hand—into whatever kind of water I found nearby. I've hauled dogfish straight up through twenty fathoms of salt water, hand over hand, and cast tiny dry flies with slender bamboo rods over dimpling brown trout with undifferentiated pleasure. My fishing experiences were at once parochial and eclectic: I rarely ventured beyond the borders of my New England, but whatever swam in our waters was fair and desirable game.

Two contrary changes are occurring. More and more I yearn for far-flung places to explore. Whereas once I lived for the stolen afternoon or evening when I could toss a rod into the car and seize a few hours of solitude beside a local brook or pond, now I plot two-week adventures a day's airplane ride away.

As the New England boundaries of my angling world have melted away, so has my undiscriminating passion for catching on hook and line all creatures that swim.

Introduction

When I'm having it my way, I fish for trout. With flies. In moving water. Preferably in faraway rivers.

When I can't do that, I fish for something else with flies.

Or I fish for trout with something other than flies.

Or I fish for trout with flies in New England.

Oh, I still like to spend a day aboard *Amethyst* with Ben Tribken, trolling forty miles offshore for albacore and yellowfin or casting poppers into schools of blues in the rips off the Vineyard. I still hope one day to tie into a giant bluefin on Tim Mahoney's *Leprechaun*. I'd consider it a lost year if Dad and I didn't troll streamers for landlocked salmon for at least one afternoon the week after ice-out on Winnipesaukee. Andy and I invest a few summer evenings paddling around our local ponds in our float tubes for largemouths, and when the bass refuse to cooperate we don't mind tying on tiny poppers and catching a mess of bluegills.

At least once a year I still dig a canful of worms and sit on the bank of the millpond near my house in suburban Massachusetts, waiting for a yellow perch or a horned pout to come along and jiggle my red-and-white bobber.

Hell, I'd rather catch eels with a handline off a Cape Cod bridge than lie around on the beach.

But it's not the same anymore. It's not fly casting for trout out West.

I'm not particularly proud of the fisherman I seem to have become. In spite of the vague sense of superiority I occasionally recognize in myself when I see somebody heaving a Mepps spinner toward a pod of rising trout, when I know he's got it all wrong, that the only kind of spinner that'll work is a #18 Rusty Spinner fished on a 6X tippet with a down-and-across drag-free drift—in spite of that, I know there's no particular virtue in my narrowed-down and rigidly ordered hierarchy of angling values.

I feel sorry for those souls who come to fishing late, who begin with fly-casting and entomology lessons at Orvis or L. L. Bean and whose first rod is a 5-weight high-modulus Sage graphite and whose first attempt to catch a fish occurs at the Battenkill. They deprive themselves of all the pleasures of getting there, and I cannot believe they will ever properly appreciate the place where they have arrived, however competent they become.

I've never attended a fishing school. On the other hand, my whole life has been an angling apprenticeship. My mentor, my father, taught me most of what I now know, both about how to catch fish and how to value the experience—which after all these years still amounts, I estimate, to less than one-tenth of what he knows about it. Our fishing trips are mainly ceremonial now—trolling for landlocks or bugging for smallmouths along the shorelines of New Hampshire's Lake Winnipesaukee, an afternoon's canoe float down the Pine River looking for rising brookies. I still learn something new every time.

I've enjoyed passing some of this along to my children, and if they so far lack the passion for fishing I had at their ages, they have been receptive and tolerant of their old man's unnatural enthusiasms. And they've taught me some things, too.

I've felt for a long time that such a consuming preoccupation as I've had with fishing sets me apart from my nonangling peers. I've got something on them, I feel, though I know better than to take any credit for it. Most of them seem to me to lack any kind of real passion whatsoever in their lives, and in their presence I feel both self-conscious and quietly superior. They are, I think, jealous, and I don't blame them. Fishing, to a great extent, defines me. A lot of people I know seem to lack definition.

I've found myself pondering all this stuff ever since I started fishing with Andy Gill. Before Andy, I mostly just fished and liked it. Now I fish and like it and wonder why. Andy's a psychiatrist. Although he tends to be hard on himself, he's scrupulous about not analyzing me. Still, in his presence I can't resist applying the textbook things I learned a long time ago.

I recall, for example, that Freud defined normality as the ability to love and work. Well, I love fishing and work very hard at it. It's comforting to know that this is normal.

Freud also said that everyone is neurotic, which is a vast relief.

One August day a couple summers ago Andy and I were casting to very spooky rainbows in a deadwater slough on a western spring creek. I was having no luck whatsoever. Andy seemed to be playing a fish all the time. This was not unusual. Andy is a more competent angler than I am, and I tend to attribute his success to his skill and leave it at that.

But when he's catching them and I'm not, part of me always believes that he has solved a mystery, and if I only knew how, I'd catch as many fish as he does. So on that day I yelled over to him, "Hey! What's your secret?"

When he answered, his voice had a manic edge to it. "Beetlemania!" he shouted.

I tied on a deerhair beetle and caught a couple myself. So I became afflicted by that peculiar angler's neurosis that we call Beetlemania, which Andy later defined as an unnaturally intense desire to fish for trout with artificial beetles. Andy further opined that Beetlemania was the ideal antidote for another fly fisherman's psychological ailment, which he has dubbed "Pattern Anxiety" (the certainty that the fly one is using is the wrong one, usually associated with a neurotic compulsion to change flies every third cast, thereby spending more time poking invisible leader tippets through invisible hook eyes than actually fishing).

Neither Pattern Anxiety nor Beetlemania, said Andy, should be confused with Nymphomania, although there are times when a little Pheasant Tail, bounced through riffles . . .

Thus began our effort to compile a taxonomy of angling neuroses, those manias and phobias, anxieties and complexes, that are peculiar to fishermen. We have barely scratched the surface.

The other day, for example, Andy called me on the phone. We had just returned from our annual fish-til-you-puke swing though Montana. "Remember that last evening on the Bighorn?" he said.

Of course I remembered. Very large brown trout were churning the surface trying to eat the black caddisflies that swarmed in the dusk. I had busted off my last caddis imitation on a fish I wish I could have seen. It was too dark to tie on another, even if I'd had one. I squatted on the bank with our guide, Bill Rohrbacher, watching Andy cast to an especially large trout he had located.

Bill turned to me and said, "He'd stay out there all night, wouldn't he?"

I nodded. I would have, too, if I could've tied on another fly.

"If you guys want to get back while the restaurant's open, we should head out soon. We got a five-mile row ahead of us."

"You tell him," I said. "Maybe he'll listen to you."

"Ten more casts, Doc," yelled Bill. "Then we're leaving, with or without you."

I heard Andy mutter, "Aw, jeez . . ."

He wrapped his fly around his rod tip on the next cast.

The one after that landed in a tangle in front of him.

Then on his backcast he hooked the tree that he had managed to avoid for an hour.

He busted it off, reeled in, and sloshed to shore. "I don't understand it," he said. "I was casting great until you gave me ten more casts."

"I remember," I said to Andy on the phone.

"As soon as Bill told me I had ten casts, I got all tense. Couldn't cast beyond my nose without messing up."

"I noticed," I said. "We were getting hungry."

"As soon as anyone rations out my casts like that, I become a bundle of uncoordinated nerves."

"I do that, too," I said, in what I hoped was a shrinklike tone.

"Well," he said, "I finally got it diagnosed."

"I bet you do."

"Simple," he said. "I suffer from a Cast Ration Complex."

I hung up on him.

To nonfishermen, fishing seems eccentric and pointless, if not downright disturbed. "You waste so much time, not to mention money . . ." And, "How can you go to so much trouble to catch a few slimy little fish, *and then you throw them back!*"

To fellow anglers, on the other hand, it's all normal and healthy. I have come to believe that the healthiest and most normal things we can do are, in fact, eccentric and pointless. For such is life in general. This book is an attempt to justify this belief.

Part 1
THE OPENING DAY
ANXIETY

I grew up in suburban Massachusetts, where I had very few friends who fished. None of them fished obsessively. So it was natural that they would consider my behavior bizarre and me a nut. After a while, I believed them. "Neurotic" was the diagnosis of a cute little redhead named Sharon, who admitted that she used to like me until she saw me on my bike one morning, hunched single-mindedly over the handlebars, ignoring her wave, my battered old bamboo fly rod squeezed against the handgrip and poking in front like some knight-in-training's flimsy lance, hellbent, obviously, on some insane quixotic mission. Sharon's old man was a professor of psychology, so I figured she probably knew what she was talking about. I accepted the label.

I fished all the time. I preferred fishing to baseball and ice cream and Sharon. I fished anywhere I could get to by bicycle. No body of water was too shallow or muddy or smelly to pass up. I lusted for Ritz-cracker sunfish and finger-sized yellow perch. My hands were chronically infected from the stab wounds of baby horned pout.

1

I discovered exotic places, too—a pond stocked with hatchery trout, a municipal water reservoir (where fishing, boating, swimming, and other forms of trespassing were forbidden) that held largemouth bass, a little coldwater rill that meandered through a swamp where tiny native brookies lived. Catching these fish in these places simply made me more neurotic.

But my compulsion to fish was nothing compared to the anxieties of not being able to fish. Back then, the season opened on April 15 and closed on September 30. No exceptions for prepubescent boys interested in stunted panfish. My attitude toward The Law was as pragmatic as that of any boy. But my respect for fish and game laws was absolute. Lobbing a gob of worms into the forbidden reservoir didn't bother me. But fishing out of season—never.

Many of the other kids, those nonobsessive sometime anglers, went fishing whenever they felt like it. Not me. I honored the season. This further confirmed old Sharon's diagnosis, in both my friends' minds and my own.

So it was logical that my worst, most neurotically obsessive time, was the couple months that preceded Opening Day. When I told my chums about it, they thought they understood. They all skipped school for the Red Sox's first appearance at Fenway. After a long deprived winter, they lusted to see Jimmy Piersall run one down in right center field, Frank Malzone spear a hotshot behind the bag, the Splendid Splinter whack a majestic drive into the visitor's bullpen.

No, I told them. That wasn't it. What I yearned for was the first twitch at the tip of my rod, the slow slither of line through the guides, the tiny tuggings of the season's first horned pout.

I still do. Sharon was right.

OPENING DAY

You wait, squatting, your arms folded across your chest, your hands tucked into your armpits. Your breath comes and goes in visible puffs.. Snowflakes the size of dimes drift from a leaden sky. Your old fiberglass fly rod rests propped at the edge of the pond in the fork of a fresh-cut stick. An extra yard of slack lies coiled on the ground.

You wait. You stare at the line where it emerges from the tip. You stand up and pace in small circles, flapping your arms against the chill. You return to squat by your rod.

Impatient now, you lift the rod and strip in line. You check your bait. Although the three worms on the hook are still squirming, you pluck them off anyway and rebait. You roll-cast the gob into the pond and set your rod back on its makeshift holder.

And you wait.

The line twitches. Or do you imagine it? You lift the rod and point the tip to where the line enters the water. Yes. A twitch. Another. Slowly, slowly, the line begins to slither through the guides. Strip off another yard of slack. Wait, wait . . .

3

Now? Yes! You lift your rod, collect the slack, and strike. Your rod bows. You feel that throbbing, living weight. "Got one!" you cry. Two dozen heads turn to watch, grinning with you.

This is it. The memory of this moment has sustained you through the winter. No more waiting. The itch has been scratched.

This is Opening Day.

For me, Opening Day was always Christmas morning, my birthday, and the last day of school, all boxed, wrapped, and beribboned into one tantalizing package that wore a tag reading, "Do Not Open Before April 15." In the rhythm of my year, the excitement of the weeks preceding Opening Day grew in a gentle crescendo, building to the high note of The Day itself. The anticipation was as delicious as the fulfillment.

Opening Day preparations began on New Year's Day with the ceremonial unwrapping of the year's new fishing calendar. I flipped through to April and crayoned in red a circle around the number 15.

Through the snows and thaws of winter I honed hooks, oiled reels, rewound guides, buffed sparkle into spinners and spoons, spun feather and fur onto hooks, detected and repaired pinholes in waders and boots, reread Edmund Ware Smith's One-Eyed Poacher tales, and excavated memories from the skeletal statistics in my old fishing log.

April 15 was, of course, a random, arbitrary date, determined long ago, no doubt, by some minor government bureaucrat. But for me as a kid, and perhaps even more so later, as a young adult, it held magical powers.

My angling appetites were more catholic in those days. Dry

fly or Jitterbug, living worm or plastic, freshwater or salt, blue-fish or bluegill, alone or with an amiable companion or two, it was all fishing and it was all fun in its own way.

But Opening Day was not mere fishing. It was a holiday, a celebration, a ritual.

Opening Day meant trout at Walden Pond. Nothing else would do.

On April 14 I dug the worms—dozens and dozens of worms. I never felt I had enough. Because Opening Day, unlike all the rest, meant lobbing a big gob of worms into Walden's icy waters and waiting for a freshly stocked rainbow trout to cruise by and pick it up. The new season arrived officially the first time the line began to jerk and slink through the guides.

Like other important holidays, and unlike all other fishing days, Opening Day was a communal occasion, a pagan revel. It was meant to be shared—not just with a special partner, or even with a group of convivial companions, but with hordes of like-minded celebrants. Walden was the place for that.

I set the alarm early on Opening Day eve. Not that it was necessary. I never slept on that night.

In the gray, predawn twilight I hid my bike in the bushes, hurried down the hill, and laid claim to a few precious feet of shoreline.

Henry David Thoreau celebrated the tranquil solitude of his Walden. Over the years there have been disciples of his who would ban swimmers, nature lovers, and fishermen from the shores of his pond as a way of sustaining his spirit.

They miss the point. I believe Thoreau would have loved the vibrant, egalitarian democracy of Walden Pond on Opening Day. Next to the L. L. Bean-clad old gentleman casting nymphs with his split-bamboo Leonard stood a boy flailing his dad's steel telescope rod. There were old-timers with rusty bait-

5

casting outfits, crude-talking men heaving two-ounce sinkers out of sight with surf-casting gear, and teenagers twirling hand-lines wrapped around soft-drink cans. Children chased dogs, and dogs chased children, and inevitably all fell in. Portable radios blared the music of drummers far different from those Thoreau marched to. Lines tangled. Shouts of "I got one!" echoed across the water. Sodden tree branches were dredged up from Walden's depths. Hands were warmed over scattered fires. Hot dogs were roasted on sticks. Coffee was shared among folks who never bothered introducing themselves.

Fingers grew numb. Rainwater dripped between collar and neck. Complaints took the form of good-natured jokes. Opening Day at Walden was a transcendent experience. Thoreau would have enjoyed it. I know I did.

Oh, yes. We caught trout. Hatchery-reared, confused and hungry, pale and scrawny, the little brookies and rainbows prowled and ate, democratically blind to artifice or refinement. Handliner, surf caster, and fly rodder all caught their share. Many a boy—including me—heaved the first trout of his life onto Walden's banks on Opening Day.

I broke the ritual a couple of times, hoping for something even better. Once I pedaled for half the morning so I could stand up to my armpits in the high, roily waters of the Squannicook River flipping spinning lures, and another time I scouted out an unnamed rill flowing through a swamp that held little native brookies.

But it wasn't the same. Those departures from tradition were like Christmas without a tree. Opening Day, for me, belonged to Walden with my great extended family of fishermen, and I kept returning there on April 15.

And then abruptly, without warning, it all changed. The Massachusetts Division of Fisheries and Wildlife decided to give us year-round fishing. No closed season. Fish anytime you want. Panfish, trout, bass, whatever you want.

No more Opening Day.

It seemed like a good idea. Natural reproduction occurs rarely in my Massachusetts trout waters. When the fishing is put-and-take, it makes sound economic sense for the take to equal the put. Trout should be caught by the folks whose taxes and license fees pay for the fishes' upbringing. A year-round open season would give us golden autumn afternoons on our ponds and rivers. It would make it possible to haul monster browns through the ice. Special regulations would still protect the sea-run trout and other targeted fisheries.

Panfish and bass could take care of themselves.

Best of all, or so it seemed, we no longer would have to wait for April 15 to arrive before we could unlimber our rods, step into our waders, and scratch that Opening Day itch. We could bounce worms through pools of surging frigid streams or troll streamers in ice-rimmed ponds as early as the spirit moved us— or at least as soon as the hatchery trucks had made their deliveries.

So why did I feel cheated?

They gave us year-round fishing, but they robbed us of Opening Day. It was not a good deal.

A few years ago I opened the trout season with a goal-oriented cluster of graphite-rodded, neoprene-wadered men standing waist-deep in the Y Pool of the Swift River. The water temperature was thirty-eight degrees. It was February 19. Around noon I landed a sixteen-inch rainbow trout on a weighted Pheasant Tail nymph. The nearby fishermen appeared to resent my triumph. I quit early.

In 1983, according to my log, I celebrated Opening Day on

January 6, bracing myself against the slashing northeast wind that cut across the iced-over surface of Walden for nine hours, waiting for a flag to pop. None did.

Last year I held out until March 22. The ice had gone out at Walden three days earlier. A taped message on the Fisheries and Wildlife phone informed me that the hatchery truck had made its delivery.

The earth in my garden had not thawed, but I found a jar of salmon eggs on the shelf of the local K-Mart. I slept soundly the night before, and I waited until the midmorning sun had taken the bite from the air before I stowed my gear in the car and set off.

There were a couple of dozen cars in the lot—not like the old days, but a good crowd. Most of the fishermen were crouched along the sand beach, a likely spot, inasmuch as it lay adjacent to the boat landing where the hatchery trucks unloaded their cargo.

I found an empty strip of sand, cut myself a forked stick, baited up, and lobbed it out there. The guy next to me lifted his eyebrows at my fly rod. He, like all the rest, had two spinning rods propped on store-bought steel holders.

"How they bitin'?" I said.

He shrugged. "Nothin'. It's fished out. Got my limit yesterday, though."

He may have been right. I squatted all day without a nibble.

When I got home, I said to my wife, "I didn't catch anything, so don't ask." I snapped off the television the kids were watching, poured myself a drink, and locked myself in my den. I had to figure it out. I'd been skunked plenty of times and still had fun. That wasn't it.

Since 1977, when the grinches stole the real one, Opening Day hasn't been the same. I've had to choose it for myself,

8

randomly, by whim, on the spur of the moment. No red-circled date on the calendar, no anticipation, no climax, no celebration.

I have made a plan. Since the law won't do it for me, and I have to do it for myself, I have decided to do it right.

Come New Year's Day, I'll unwrap my new fishing calendar and set my own Opening Day—April 15, as good a day as any.

Then I'll wait. I'll hone hooks and oil reels, tie flies and read fishing stories. When Andy and Doc call, I'll be resolute. The season isn't open yet, I'll tell them. Will power. I'll starve myself. I'll wait.

On April 14 I'll dig a canful of worms, and before bed I'll pile my gear by the back door. I'll set the alarm, but I won't sleep much.

I can feel the anticipation building, that old itch. It feels good. I won't scratch it. Not yet. I'll wait for Opening Day.

BAIT HUNTING WITH SKEETER

The only fish of significance that Skeeter Cronin or I ever caught from Mud Pond was a two-foot eel. Skeeter fooled him with a gob of dead nightcrawlers, our favorite horned-pout bait.

Mostly we snagged severely stunted sunfish and bullheads from that shallow, sunbaked ecological disaster, but it was the only fishing hole within biking distance. We carefully returned everything we caught, having read somewhere that true sportsmen practice the catch-and-release ethic. We debated keeping the eel, a trophy. We figured none of the neighborhood kids would believe us if we couldn't produce the evidence of our triumph. But neither of us volunteered to handle the twisty slimy thing, so Skeeter cut the line.

We followed a similar ethic when we hunted for bait. We caught it by hand—traps, nets, and seines we considered unsportsmanlike—and returned what we didn't use to the place where we had found it.

Although we didn't discuss it at the time, I suspect that Skeeter felt the way I did about our fishing: Catching Ritz-cracker sunfish or bullheads that looked like breakfast sausages was nowhere near as much fun as gathering bait.

Bait hunting was, for us, a sport in its own right. Fishing served as a rationalization for our sport, the same way that eating sea ducks allows the hunter to justify shooting them.

Worms, of course, were our standby, and for fish-catching purposes all we ever really needed. But gathering worms soon proved too easy and too boring to sustain our interest. We thirsted for more exotic sport.

Nightcrawler hunting, we discovered, provided the adventure and challenge we sought.

Normally my mother didn't allow me out after dark on my bike in the summer. When Skeeter and I had a plan to gather nightcrawlers, however, she made an exception. She was married to a fisherman, after all, so she understood sporting priorities. On the evening of a nightcrawler hunt, I wrapped red cellophane over the lens of my flashlight, securing it with an elastic band, and pedaled over to Skeeter's. He was responsible for providing the coffee can. Then we biked to the golf course. The seventh fairway ran parallel to the road, and the sprinklers came on at dusk. After the turf got soaked, the crawlers began to poke their heads out of their holes.

Skeeter and I convinced each other that the groundskeeper kept a shotgun loaded with rock salt handy to chase off trespassers, especially those bent on swiping nightcrawlers, so we hid our bikes in the bushes and made quick evasive forays onto the fairway when we figured the coast was clear. That groundskeeper never did catch us.

Nightcrawlers, we found, were blessed with quick reflexes and cursed with soft musculature. Grab one too gingerly and it snapped back into its hole. Grab and yank too hard and it busted in half. The best technique, we discovered, was to seize it behind the head and hold it firmly for a moment until it relaxed. Then it could be eased from its hole and deposited into the coffee can.

We always returned home after our normal bedtimes, stinking of nightcrawler slime, soaked and muddy from the sprinklers, and wired on the thrill of the hunt.

Live nightcrawlers were about twice as long as the fish we hoped to catch with them, and they turned out to be poor bait. We preferred them to worms, nevertheless, because they were great fun to hunt. We never tired of outwitting that evil old groundskeeper.

Dead nightcrawlers, it turned out, fooled horned pout regularly. We discovered this marvelous bait accidentally, when Skeeter's mother dragged him off to shop for school clothes one morning after we had filled a coffee can at the golf course. Skeeter had left the can of crawlers beside his garage, where the sun beat on it for two days. When we finally got fishing, we found our coffee can was filled with smelly slimy gunk. But we crammed the stuff onto a hook anyway. The pouts loved it, and so did that trophy eel.

Skeeter and I were always on the lookout for new baits. Their fish-catching potential intrigued us less than the possibility of discovering a new bait-catching sport. We tried all manner of caterpillars, but they weren't much good. Too easy to catch, for one thing. They also squirted venomous green juice at us when we stuck a hook into them.

Skeeter's old man put us onto slugs. "Excellent bait, slugs," he assured us. He suggested we set out shallow saucers of beer in his vegetable garden under the tomato plants to trap them. "Slugs love beer," he told us. "They'll crawl into the saucer and get plastered. Then they're easy pickin's." He tipped up the beer can he was holding, drained half of it, and handed it to Skeeter. "This," he said pointedly, "is for catching slugs, boys."

At first we resisted using beer-baited traps. "We catch all our bait by hand," Skeeter told his old man. "It's the right way to do it."

12

When Mr. Cronin said he'd give us a nickel for every dozen slugs we captured, we reluctantly modified our ethics and trapped a quarter's worth in two nights.

We found that neither sunfish nor horned pout cared much for slugs, so we returned what we hadn't used to Mr. Cronin's garden. Skeeter later told me that his old man was demanding his quarter back.

One summer evening Skeeter called me on the phone and whispered, "Crawdads."

"What about 'em?"

"Bass bait. I just read about it in one of my old man's magazines."

"There's no bass in Mud Pond, Skeets."

"There might be. We'll never know if we don't try for 'em with proper bass bait."

It was unassailable logic. I had trouble sleeping that night, anticipating the adventures that awaited me.

Crawfish turned out to be marvelous prey—scarce, hard to see, elusive, wary. We took off our shoes and socks, rolled up our pantslegs, and waded the shallow gravel-bottomed end of Mud Pond. Crawdads, we learned, possessed lightning reflexes. They darted around in little puffs of mud quicker than we could grab them. Once we figured out that they traveled backwards, we did manage to hand-capture a few of them.

Skeeter said he had read that if you remove the top and bottom of a two-pound coffee can you can slip it over a crawdad and then easily reach in and get him. Even though we had violated our no-trap ethic on slugs, we decided that crawfish were noble quarry, deserving only the most sporting tactics. We'd catch 'em by hand, or we wouldn't catch 'em at all.

After his marvelous discovery of crawfish, Skeeter scoured the pages of his old man's magazines, seeking new offbeat bait-hunting challenges. We yearned for a cold running stream where we might hunt hellgrammites and caddis larvae. We resigned ourselves to waiting until we were older before we'd be able to pursue exotic species such as hellgrammites in far-flung places.

I read a story by some famous writer about how much fun he had catching grasshoppers. You had to get up early, which appealed to me and Skeeter, in order to get 'em while their wings were still damp from dew and they couldn't fly. The problem with hoppers was that they were only good on trout streams, and we knew of no trout streams within biking distance. We did capture a canful of grasshoppers one morning anyway, and we kept them for a while before we let them go. That writer was right. It was excellent sport. The way he wrote about catching trout with them sounded pretty good, too.

If the grasshopper was the prince of insect baits, then the cricket, Skeeter and I agreed, was the king. We found prime cricket terrain in the field adjacent to the lumberyard near Skeeter's house. Old planks lay scattered on the ground. Under each plank hid crickets—sometimes as many as a dozen under an especially good plank. Crickets far surpassed damp-winged grasshoppers in elusiveness. They hopped in unpredictable directions, much the way a grouse bursts from a thicket, and our reflexes were tested to their fullest when we tried to trap one under the palms of our hands.

There were two particular challenges to hand-trapping a cricket: When we lifted a hand to verify that we had captured one, he tended to hop away; and, if he didn't hop away, we were likely to find a squashed cricket.

A single cricket, impaled on a small hook, turned out to be excellent sunfish bait, a bonus for me and Skeeter. We only used them a few times, however. We didn't admit it to each other, but I think Skeeter agreed with me that there was something lovable about crickets that made us uncomfortable stick-ing hooks into them.

We had the same attitude toward leopard frogs, which were probably our favorite bait to hunt and the one we most disliked actually fishing with. To hunt frogs, one of us would wade calf-deep in the water along the bank of Mud Pond while the other kept pace on the shore, spotting and flushing our quarry. Usu-ally the frog would leap toward the wader. Occasionally he ac-tually caught one. There were better ways to catch frogs, but Skeeter and I were purists, so we allowed ourselves to use only our hands.

We caught very few frogs, and we released them all. But frog hunting indirectly taught us about leech hunting, and leech hunting, in its turn, produced the first real disagreement on the ethics of our sport that Skeeter and I had.

It happened on that particular summer afternoon that Skeeter was up to his knees in Mud Pond, trying to catch frogs, and I was on shore bird-dogging for him. After perhaps an hour of near captures, Skeeter waded out. "I haven't got the hang of it today," he said. "You take a turn."

I glanced at him. "Hey, look!" I said, pointing at his bare legs.

They were spotted with leeches—bloodsuckers, we called them.

Skeeter began to leap around, swatting at his legs.

"Wait," I said. "Let me get a can."

"What for?"

"I read somewhere that bloodsuckers are terrific bait."

We plucked about a dozen leeches off Skeeter's calves. Then I said, "Okay. Wade back in there. Let's get more."

Skeeter shook his head. "No way."

"Chicken?"

"Hell, no. It's just not the right way. Baiting your bait is not moral."

"What are you talking about?"

"You want to use my legs for bloodsucker bait. That's wrong."

"It's not the same thing. You're just afraid of them."

He shook his head. "Nope. It's plain immoral."

I thought for a minute. "Okay, then," I said, shucking off my sneakers. "I'll do it."

Skeeter spotted the trap. He hesitated only an instant before he said, "No. It's wrong. Either way, it's wrong."

We never did test the effectiveness of bloodsuckers as bait.

After high school, Skeeter and I lost touch with each other, although I got a Christmas card from him several years ago. He said he had become bitten with the fly-fishing bug.

Then last summer I ran into him at our high school reunion. Never mind which one. We found a corner table, fortified ourselves with gin and tonics, and reminisced about fishing in Mud Pond and the great bait-hunting expeditions we had shared as kids. He told me how he had finally gotten the chance to seine hellgrammites in Maine when he was in college. I expressed envy, then chided him for not using his bare hands. He admitted that he had felt badly about using unsportsmanlike methods. But he did catch an admirable stringer of smallmouth bass.

I asked him if he was still hooked on fly fishing.

"Actually, I haven't been fishing for several years," he replied. "As soon as I took up serious fly fishing, I began to tie flies. A couple years later I gave away all my rods. Found I didn't have time for fishing. Too busy tying flies."

I nodded. Somehow it didn't surprise me.

TRICKLE TROUT

After three days of dragging streamer flies around New Hampshire's Lake Winnipesaukee without a strike, Doc called a council of war.

"The way I see it," he said, "we can continue to not catch landlocked salmon, or we can go get a couple limits of trout."

"Aw," I said, "I really don't feel like fighting for elbow room just to catch a bunch of limp hatchery rainbows."

"The big lake has hardly given us a wilderness experience," he said. "Besides," he added with a familiar glint in his eye, "I got an idea."

I shrugged. I'd follow Doc's lead. Generally his ideas were good ones.

So we threw his little thirteen-foot Grumman atop his Jeep and headed into the woods. A paved road led to a dirt road, which took us to a pair of old ruts. A mile or so farther on Doc stopped and we climbed out.

We dragged the little canoe through alders and around blowdown until we came upon a brook I could almost have stepped over, an unimpressive little rill that seemed to disappear into the swampy undergrowth.

17

I braced my hands on my hips. "You kidding?" I said.

He grinned. "Trust me."

So we loaded a paddle, a pushpole, an ultralight spinning rod, a seven-foot fly rod, and a bag of assorted gear into the canoe. Then we pulled on our hip boots. We were about to climb in when Doc snapped his fingers. "Almost forgot," he said.

He went back to the Jeep and returned a moment later with the pair of heavy-duty loppers he uses to prune his fruit trees. "We'll need these," he said.

He put me in the bow, armed with the loppers, and he took the stern. Alternately poling and paddling, he pushed us slowly upstream. I put the loppers to good use in several places where the alders crowded the narrow banks. In places the brook was barely as wide as the canoe. Several times I had to climb out to drag us over blowdown or shallows.

But here and there the brook widened into slow pools, and then Doc held the canoe while I probed the undercut banks and boulders and sunken trees with the little spinning outfit. And it seemed that every likely looking spot held trout. They were gorgeous fat little orange-bellied native brookies with spots like drops of fresh blood. They struck hard and willingly, although several times I saw shadows dart ahead of us when we approached too boldly.

They ran small—six to nine inches—and achieving a cast that landed in the water rather than the alders tested the limits of my rusty spin-casting skills. It was fortunate—or good planning—that Doc had brought plenty of the tiny gold Panther Martin spinners, because I left half a dozen of them in the brush or on underwater stubs.

A mile or so upstream we came upon a beaver dam. "Fresh cuttings," observed Doc. "Good. Old beaver ponds get silty and acid, but this one looks recent. It'll hold trout."

18

The pond was no bigger than Doc's living room. But we spotted five separate trout rising to a sparse hatch of large yellowish mayflies. "Look," I said. "Yellow mayflies."

Doc muttered something in Latin.

"What'd you say?"

"Medical school talk," he said. "It means yellow mayflies."

He assembled his fly rod and tied on a Royal Wulff. "They ain't particular," he said. "If they're rising, they'll take anything that'll float." Crouching behind the dam, he roll-cast to the risers and caught three of them before the others decided something dangerous was happening in their little sanctuary.

On the way downstream we swapped ends. We had just pushed through an especially dense alder thicket when Doc held up his hand. "Riser," he whispered. "Good one, too."

The trout was holding about thirty feet downstream from us, hard against the bank and under some brush that canopied his lie. "Forget it," I said. "You'll never get a fly to him."

"Oh, yeah?"

Doc made a little fifteen-foot roll cast, and then shook some slack line out of his rod. I watched the white-winged Wulff bounce and drift along the current. Doc wiggled more line from his rod tip. The fly approached the lair of the trout as Doc's line began to straighten. He leaned forward, thrusting his rod ahead of him to extend his float. Then I heard him grunt as the Wulff disappeared in a heavy swirl. His rod came up bowed.

I glimpsed a quick flash of orange as the brookie rolled at the surface. Then Doc's rod straightened.

"Nuts," he said, stripping in his slack line. This, for Doc, was a serious curse. "Snagged me. Big trout, too. Twelve, thirteen inches, at least."

Do you like wide open spaces? Do you define good fishing as heaving big lures out of sight or demonstrating the double haul with your 8-weight graphite fly rod? Do you define a trout as a fish raised in a cement tub, fed on high-protein pellets until it's a foot long, then trucked to a place where it might be caught? Do you enjoy sitting by a pond or river and chatting with strangers? Do you go fishing to relax and get some sunshine?

If your answer is yes to any or all of these questions, then fishing the trickles is probably not for you.

Doc and I love it, but then, most people think Doc and I are strange. Oh, like most trout addicts, we spend outrageous amounts of tuition and food money on airplane trips to distant places where fabled rivers flow big and powerful and great trout gobble tiny flies. We love the Bighorn and the Bow and the Green and the others.

But at least once in the early New England season, while most other anglers follow the hatchery trucks to the well-known trout spots, Doc and I seek out our roots. We scout the nameless little feeder streams that meander as thin blue lines on our topographic maps. Some of them bubble quick and riffly down rocky mountainsides, pooling at boulder-strewn levels to gather momentum for the next descent. Others meander slowly and aimlessly through swamp and meadow. Many of them we can cross in a walking stride. Others, we have to take a running leap.

Not all of them, of course, hold trout. But many do, and when Doc and I find one, the thrill of discovery almost equals the fun of catching the fish.

We're after brookies, the only trout indigenous to the Northeast—not the pallid imitations raised by the Fish and Game folks for general consumption, but true natives, descendants of those that the original Americans were catching when this land was labeled Terra Incognita by European cartographers. Brook trout, ironically, are less hardy than their imported cousins, the rainbow and the brown. They demand colder, cleaner water, an increasingly scarce resource in these days of industrial, highway, and residential sprawl.

For these reasons, Doc and I regard them, and the trickles where they still swim, as treasures, and we treat them as such. Small brooks live on an ecological knife edge. In addition to the invasions of bulldozers—too many of my once-favorite trout trickles now flow between concrete banks—fishing pressure can affect trout life in little brooks more severely than in big waters. Can a brook be fished out? You bet it can, if too many people fish it too hard and without concern for the limitations of the resource. Likewise, underfishing can produce an excess population of stunted trout. So Doc and I determine the numbers and sizes of the trout we bring home from brook fishing by the needs of the place rather than the needs of the frying pan.

One rule of thumb we always follow, whether or not we want to bring home a brace of breakfast brookies: We always return the larger breeder fish, which we define as anything longer than ten inches.

Fishing for native brookies in trickles is more than just an offbeat way of recapturing a glimpse of our youth. In the frigid waters of April it can be the only sport. There are two reasons for this: Brook trout become active earlier than their warmer-blooded brown and rainbow relations; and small, shallow waters tend to warm up quicker than big rivers or ponds. Thus we often find that in the early season our only alternative to sulking, sluggish hatchery trout is hungry little native brookies in their natural habitat. For Doc and me, there's no problem making that choice.

There are several effective methods for fishing the trickles. Our method is determined largely by the nature of the water. Wherever casting is possible, Doc and I prefer to use flies.

Brookies love bright little drys or wets or small streamers—especially, for some reason, red-and-white patterns. They gobble bushy nymphs eagerly. We don't have to cast far, but we have to cast accurately. Most of our fly casting on trickle trout is of the roll-cast variety, often from awkward kneeling or crouching postures. Sometimes we have to poke our rods through the bushes and dap a fly from only a few feet of leader. In places we can drift a nymph or bushy dry down to likely fish lairs.

Ultralight spinning, with four-foot rods and four-pound monofilament, was made for small brooks, and brookies love flashy spinners and fingernail-sized red-and-white wobblers. Gold spinners are especially effective when the water is high and discolored. In early season, when even brookies lie lethargically on the bottom of the deep runs, an upstream cast retrieved bumping the bottom often takes reluctant trout. We're always prepared to lose some lures. We know if we're not getting down among the sunken snags, we're not where the fish are.

Doc and I are neither proud nor rigid. It's true that we love feathers and fur and the lovely grace of the fly rod best of all, and on our beloved western rivers we wouldn't consider any alternative. But we learned long ago that the best method for taking trickle trout is usually on a drifted worm, either lobbed with an ultralight spinning rod or, preferably, drifted from a fly rod. It was good enough for us as kids, and it's good enough now. Brookies eat worms under almost any water conditions, although on rising water during or soon after a spring storm they are extra voracious. Worm-fishing the trickles is not for the lazy. Natural presentation is the key. A lightly impaled squirming worm on a small hook with a drag-free drift makes all the difference.

Worming the trickles requires the same delicate precision as floating a #20 Pale Morning Dun over the nose of a sipping Henry's Fork rainbow. The worm must be steered into the deep holes against undercut banks, under streamside shrubbery, and along the edges of submerged logs and boulders. We read the water. We look for feeding lanes, shelter, breaks in the current. In this respect, the trickles are no different from their oversized cousins. The harder it is to fish the spot, the better it's likely to be. After all, these are the places that most other fishermen pass up, or at best fish ineffectively. They also seem to be the spots that the fish favor. We prefer to cast upstream so that the worm sinks and tumbles naturally, without extra weight if possible, or with a pinched-on single split shot if necessary. Doc and I always tie a 4X tippet onto the ends of our leaders. We know that if we're fishing right we're going to snag bottom, and we'd rather break off easily and sacrifice a few hooks than disturb a good pool.

Doc and I probe otherwise inaccessible swamp and deep-forest trickles from his little canoe. But we prefer to prowl our trickles clad in hip boots. When fishing together, we leapfrog each other. I'll start in and Doc will move forty or fifty yards upstream from me. He'll hang his red kerchief on a bush at the place he begins fishing. When I fish up to the kerchief, I'll take it and walk upstream another forty or fifty yards beyond Doc and hang the kerchief there.

By canoe or afoot, Doc and I have learned that stealth is the single most vital skill of the trickle stalker. Native brookies usually are not hard to catch—provided we haven't spooked them. It may be one reason we like to fish in places where other fishermen don't go: We don't want anyone to see us acting foolish. We hunker down, we crawl on hands and knees, we get wet and muddy. We hardly ever actually step into the brook.

Everything in the trickles is in miniature—the brook itself, the fish that live in it (although sometimes we've been pleasantly surprised), the gear, and the lies that hold fish. In proportion, mistakes are magnified. The flash of a waving rod, a booted foot kicking a rock, the misplaced splash of a lure, the sudden appearance of a mud cloud in the water, all frighten native brookies who survive by being alert to natural dangers.

In a pool the size of a bathtub, the trout may hold in a lie the size of a dinner plate. Unless the lure or bait reaches his plate, he will not eat. This means that trickles must be closely read. Two dozen random drifts or casts in a pool may produce nothing except a hookup on a snag and spooked trout, while a single, carefully conceived and executed presentation will usually catch the trout that lives there.

Doc and I have discovered these trickles by following tributaries upstream from larger trout rivers or tracing the inlets to ponds. We have stumbled upon them while exploring woodcock covers in the autumn. We have prospected the thinnest blue lines on topographic maps. We have braved mosquito and blackfly and swamp mud. The tougher the trek, the better we like it. Our beloved trickles, like our angling roots, are hidden and elusive.

We recognize that these little brooks and the native trout that live in them are rapidly vanishing resources, so we treat them with respect and hoard them like misers.

And we fish them with love.

Part 2
THE DEPTH WISH

I've fallen into some of the finest trout rivers in the United States, and plenty of lesser ones as well. The Box Canyon—well, everyone takes a tumble there sooner or later. The first time I went after shad on the Indianhead I skidded on my butt, otterlike, down a mud bank up to my chin into it before I even had a chance to cast a fly. I've stepped up to my hat into a dozen hidden potholes in the Ipswich where it wanders through the marsh. I once stumbled on a boulder and floated fifty feet downstream in the Deerfield, playing a nice fourteen-inch brown the whole way. I've sloshed water over the tops of my waders in just about every western river I've come within a mile of. It's become a baptismal ritual for me. Until I've dunked myself, I haven't properly communed with the place.

Sometimes it's the result of careless wading. More often I know exactly what I'm doing. I watch the water rise around my waders as I edge forward, a cautious step at a time, probing with my toe for rocks, finding the depth, testing it. Thigh, hip, belly button, sternum. Every inch forward gets me that much closer to the trout I want, the one that always rises just beyond my modest casting range. The first trickle comes in the back, where my waders sag and where I can't see, while I still have a comfortable half-inch in front.

So I usually come home wet, reaffirming for me a truth about fishing that I learned a long time ago: The trout I *really* want to catch always lies just out of range, unless I'm willing to wade in beyond my depth.

Which I always am.

This, of course, is a truth about life in general, too, and, according to Andy, a truth about me, although I have no intention of analyzing that one too closely.

My depth wish translates, metaphorically at least, into a compulsion to cast to truly faraway fish. They're always bigger and stronger and the waters where they live are always more beautiful than those close to home. When I was a kid, limited by the range of my three-speed Raleigh, I dreamed of motoring to Vermont's Otter Creek and Maine's Grand Lake Stream. When those came within reach, I began to look beyond them.

Now I've fished some of the storied rivers of the West, but my friends tell me that I've still got that faraway look about me. I want to see the entire fishing world. Alaska, Argentina, New Zealand, Iceland. Are there trout streams in Egypt or Mongolia or Shangri-la? I lust to wade them all.

There are many more rivers in the world I hope to fall into before I die.

TOADS IN THE SCUMLINE

On a muggy Massachusetts afternoon several summers ago, shortly after Andy and I started fishing together, he stopped by the house. He had just returned from his annual western trout odyssey. Like Dustin Hoffman in *The Graduate*, I was beckoned close.

His secret was not plastics.

"The Bighorn," he whispered hoarsely. "The Madison, the Henry's Fork. Spring creeks. Big toads. Pods of 'em." Andy fairly fizzed with excitement. "Best trout fishin' in the lower forty-eight." He grabbed my shoulder. "You owe it to yourself. Next summer you gotta come West with me."

What weekend duffer doesn't dream of playing just one round at St. Andrews? What bathtub crooner, grooving on his own rendition of "My Way" in the hiss of his morning shower, wouldn't secretly relish the chance to bring down the house at Carnegie Hall? Is there a beer-bellied softball slugger in the land who wouldn't like to take a shot at Fenway Park's Green Monster?

More to the point: Is there a fly fisherman anywhere in the

East who doesn't yearn to pay homage to the great trout rivers of the American West?

I had been catching trout on flies for more than three decades—blood-spotted little native brookies in Maine, fat rainbows from cold running Vermont mountain streams, even an occasional big—that is, sixteen inches, maybe—brown trout.

I devoured Ted Trueblood's tales of high mountain cutthroats. I read Charles E. Brooks on the rivers of Yellowstone.

I had even been skunked on the Battenkill.

My time had come.

"Okay," I said to Andy. "This tenderfoot is going West."

We planned and plotted. I bought a new hat. I was humble. I was reverent. I was eager. I was ready.

Or so I thought. Oh, I brought along all the right equipment. Andy saw to that. My eastern skills, while crude, proved adequate. As a matter of fact, I caught plenty of trout.

What brought me down was the language barrier. I thought a PMD was some kind of doctor. *Infrequens*, I figured, described the sex life of a married trout fisherman.

In the West they use a different vocabulary. Words just don't mean the same thing out there as they do back East. Connotation versus denotation, or something.

In any case, I have decided that there's no reason why future pilgrims to trout Mecca should be as etymologically handicapped as I was. So for the benefit of those planning their first western trip—and for those who have returned from one as perplexed as I was—I have prepared a short glossary of important western words and phrases.

Tuck it in with your gear. Keep it handy for when you enter a fly shop. You don't want them to *know* you're a tenderfoot.

GUIDE: A man who charges more than *you* make in a day to row you down a river in a boat.

Western guides come in two types: good guides and bad guides. Both kinds charge about the same.

A good guide knows and loves his river and his trout and his entomology. He believes passionately in the catch-and-release credo. He has secret places he will share only with clients who believe as he does. Although he may lapse into Latin now and then, he translates willingly. He has fished all over the world, and he likes to talk about it. He's happy when his clients catch lots of big fish. He likes to teach wives and children how to cast a fly. He likes it best when they end up outfishing you. Good guides don't wear watches. They like to start earlier than you do, so that you won't miss the early hatches. Good guides often keep you out after dark, but they always know a restaurant that stays open late.

The eastern tenderfoot practices foolish economy if he fishes a strange western river without a good guide.

A bad guide rows rapidly down the middle of the river and looks at his watch a lot. The clients of bad guides are advised to take photographs of the scenery as it speeds past and not to worry about fishing. Bad guides always time it so that the boat is beached at the takeout on the nose of four in the afternoon, just when the clouds of caddis begin to show over the water.

Guides, incidentally, are also doodads on your fly rod. When you reel that carelessly tied nail knot connecting your fly line to your leader in too far and the big rainbow on the end of your line decides to make one more run for it, your guides will snap off like wood chips from a shredder. I saw this happen.

TIPS: Good guides have plenty of these, and they give them away generously. For example, Bob Lamm, a good guide, advised Andy and me to use black deerhair beetles to catch the big rainbows of the Henry's Fork, and Bill Rohrbacher, another good one, taught us how to time the rising rhythm of Bighorn brown trout. Both useful tips.

29

Good clients give tips to good guides, too. Andy and I figured 20 or 25 percent was a good tip.

Tippet is another thing. Out West, 6X is not considered flimsy. On the other hand, hamfisted eastern tenderfoots tend to bust off large trout on 6X. This is personal testimony.

LATIN: A specialized language understood by western guides, insects, trout, and eastern anglers equipped with Sage rods and Ross reels. Dave Schuller, another good Bighorn guide, speaks Latin fluently.

It is not particularly useful actually to understand Latin, nor do those who speak it seem inclined to tutor those who don't. But the eastern foreigner will feel more comfortable if he can at least tell when this language is being used. Some Latin words to recognize are: *Pseudocloeon, inermis, Tricorythodes,* and *Callibaetis.* Completely synonymous with one another, these words all mean "little bug," or mayfly in eastern parlance.

Sonofabitch is another Latin word. It means "large-brown-trout-that-just-snapped-a-6X-tippet."

TOAD: A large trout, identified by the way its toad-shaped head protrudes above the surface of the water when it eats. Also referred to as head, shark, or sonofabitch.

POD: A group of toads.

AVERAGE: A western word meaning between fifteen and sixteen inches. In eastern vocabularies, average means ten inches. Tenderfoots adjust to the western scale rapidly.

Average trout are landed as quickly as possible and released with a bored yawn. Do not photograph average trout. The appropriate benediction over an average trout is "ho hum."

Less-than-average trout are called babies, or tiddlers, or "nothing" ("What've you got?" "Nothing.") Try to avoid catching nothing. If, by mistake, you do, act embarrassed.

Toads, by definition, are above-average trout.

EMERGERS: A favorite term, probably of Latin derivation, used by guides to explain why their clients aren't catching anything. "They're feeding on PMD emergers in the film," for example. "Spinners" is another term, used for the same purpose.

GULPER: A subspecies of toad found in western lakes, characterized by its atrocious table manners.

Gulpers characteristically lift their big snouts out of the water and cruise along the surface, gobbling (*gulping,* get it?) all the little bugs, cigar butts, and #16 Adamses that lie in their path. They look exactly like Pacmen.

You catch gulpers from either a boat or a float tube. Boats equipped with electric motors offer greater mobility than tubes. On the other hand, tubes lower the fisherman's profile, allowing shorter casts to gulpers. Take your pick. I prefer the float tube.

Small flies on flimsy tippets are preferred for gulper fishing. Pattern does not seem important. Cast your dry fly in the anticipated route of your chosen gulper. Watch him approach it. Don't get excited.

I busted off a gulper in the dawn mists of Hebgen Lake because I got excited. I wasn't the only one. Bob Lamm estimated it was twenty-six inches long, and he seemed excited. Michael Enright, my companion at the time, also got excited. "Oh, a real toad," he moaned, before feigning a grand mal seizure in the bottom of the boat.

SPRING CREEK: Relatively small, cold, spring-fed, smooth-flowing rivers characterized by thick weed beds, rich trout forage, and an abundance of resident toads.

Spring creeks will not, at first, intimidate an easterner. The trout that live in them probably will.

The three spring creeks that feed the Yellowstone River in Paradise Valley near Livingston, Montana, just north of the park, (Nelson's, Armstrong's, and DePuy's) all flow through private ranchland. Landowners, who know a good thing when they see it, rent a fixed number of daily fishing rights. The price is creeping up, like everything else. It's always a bargain. Beats on the spring creeks must be booked months in advance, although if you're in the vicinity it's worth calling to see if there have been cancellations. Andy and I once lucked into a day at Armstrong's this way.

We've had marvelous fishing on spring creeks with beetles, cast down and across to steady risers. We also regularly get skunked during the evening hatch. We've been informed that they're probably eating emergers. We have been unable to verify this theory.

The Railroad Ranch section of the Henry's Fork is also a spring creek, albeit a very large one. Toads live there, too.

FREESTONE: Not a spring creek. A river bedded with slimy stones, pebbles, rocks, and boulders that tend to move under felt-soled waders (hence "free"). Freestone rivers are designed to make wading trout fishermen—with or without a depth wish—slip and stumble and fill their waders with cold water.

The Madison is a freestone river. Likewise the Box Canyon section of the Henry's Fork, where two out of every three wading fishermen fall in.

Large trout reside in the glides, riffles, and pockets of freestone rivers, which otherwise resemble many of the bigger eastern rivers familiar to you.

FLY SHOP: A place where Latin is spoken. In towns like Livingston and Last Chance and Fort Smith and West Yellowstone there are more fly shops than gas stations. A friendly thing for an easterner to say in a fly shop is: "Gimme a half dozen of everything the trout are eating these days."

Folks who work in fly shops know their bugs and their local

rivers. They give good advice, for the obvious reason. When visiting fishermen have good luck, they will return to the fly shop to buy more flies.

Besides flies, fly shops also sell rods and reels and waders and nets. Also books, paintings, sweaters, and bathing suits (not to mention ceramic ashtrays and souvenir tee shirts). Everything has a trout motif. Everything is expensive.

Guides reserved through fly shops tend to be good ones.

WIND: That which blows constantly in the face of fishermen out West.

On the Ranch, the preferred approach to a feeding trout is from above, quartering down with a reach cast and then shaking out extra slack for a long drag-free float. On the Ranch, the wind always blows upstream.

Bighorn guides Dave Schuller and Bill Rohrbacher prefer directly upriver casts, laying 6X tippet between the eyes of feeding browns. The wind always blows downstream on the Bighorn.

THE BOX: (See "Freestone") The Box Canyon section of the Henry's Fork, where it flows out of the dam at the Island Park Reservoir.

Charles E. Brooks called the Box "three miles of the best fast-water trout fishing anywhere." Box trout are shaped like footballs. Mike Lawson, who runs The Henry's Fork Anglers in nearby Last Chance, Idaho, once caught a 22½-inch rainbow that weighed 7½ pounds from the Box. Twenty-pounders have been electroshocked by biologists in the Box.

The Box can be waded, although it's a steep hike getting down into it, and even steeper getting back out after dark with waders full of water. Bring a wading staff and a dry change of clothes. It's better to hire a guide to float you through. Box currents are more powerful than a locomotive and some of its boulders are the size of a caboose. Its freestone bed is slick and treacherous. When Bob Lamm took Andy and me down the Box, he climbed out of the boat and walked us through the choice runs, qualifying him forever as a good guide.

Weighted streamers and big rubberlegs that imitate stonefly nymphs work best in the Box. Andy and I caught dozens of trout apiece there, including several that were larger than average.

CUTT: Cutthroat trout, native to the West, unknown in eastern rivers.

When we were planning our first trip, I told Andy one of my goals was to catch a cutthroat.

"Hardly a high aspiration," he said. "They're gorgeous, all right. But easy to catch. Cutts are generally considered second-class trout out West."

We floated the South Fork of the Snake for cutts one day, and on another occasion we tried them on the Yellowstone River at Buffalo Ford in the park. Cutts sport brilliant orange slashes under their jaws. They take blond Humpies eagerly and fight hard. They seem first-rate to me.

WHITEFISH: Sleek silvery fish that can be fooled with dry flies and nymphs about as easily as trout. Whitefish were short-changed in the jaw department, which probably accounts for their low reputation. I enjoy catching whitefish but will not admit it.

DOUBLE RENEGADE: The hot fly one summer in the West, it's probably extinct by now. It was recommended by fly shop personnel for catching cutts on the South Fork. It resembles the product of crossbreeding between a coral snake and a black widow spider. Worked well on whitefish.

SEVENTEEN INCHES: Slightly bigger than average. A personal benchmark. I caught at least one trout seventeen inches or longer each day of my first trip out West. There have been trips since that first one when I have not done as well.

SCUMLINE: Bighorn guide Bill Rohrbacher's term for a slick of water that funnels enormous numbers of floating insects with Latin names against the bank.

The bugs are so thick that they create a scum on the surface. Big pods of toads feed in scumlines so voraciously that you can hear them slurp and chew their food.

Andy and I once spent an entire day fishing a single Bighorn scumline no longer than a bowling alley or wider than your living room. We took turns, and between us we caught thirty-six trout, all but a couple above average.

BLOW UP: What a surface-feeding toad will do when a clumsy eastern tenderfoot drops his fly line on top of it. Resembles the commotion a muskellunge makes when it attacks a mallard.

BRUSHING THEIR TEETH: Whisking a dry fly out of the mouth of a toad before he can clamp down on it, thereby failing to hook him.

You can avoid brushing the teeth of above-average western trout by practicing a slow, deliberate strike.

I brushed the teeth of many of the toads that I had failed to blow up.

There you have it. An even twenty genuine western trout terms guaranteed to enhance your enjoyment of your trip without taking an extension course in Latin.

Oh, yes. PMD and *infrequens*. Both mean Pale Morning Dun. Little bug, or mayfly, to you.

BIGHORN OF PLENTY

From the double-ended driftboat in the middle of the river, the dimples on the slick water against the steep cliff were, to me, indistinguishable from the raindrops that pattered down softly from the iron-colored Montana sky. But guide Bill Rohrbacher pulled hard on his left oar and angled crosscurrent until the bow nosed against the bank. Bill shipped the oars and dropped the anchor.

Upstream from where we sat, little black snouts lifted rhythmically above the surface. We could actually hear them slurping.

An impish grin glinted from the tangles of Bill's black beard. "I give you," he proclaimed, "a lovely pod of large Bighorn brown trout. You want to flip for it?"

"Huh?" said Andy.

"You boys've been working your butts off all week now, the way I hear it. All wrist-cramped from hauling big trout out of places like the Henry's Fork and Hebgen Lake, the fabled Madison, spring creeks, whatever. I can see how your noses're blistered and your tender eastern lips're all chapped from our

wicked western sun. Up before dawn so as not to miss the Trico
hatch. Inhaling caddisflies after dark. At the vise into the wee
hours trying to manufacture something that'll match yesterday's
hatch. Eating guide food, like Schuller's antelope sausage,
pounding all over Idaho and Montana in that little rental car
with the bad brakes."

"I'm fine," said Andy. "Jeez, lookit those fish."

"Hang on," said Bill. "Yesterday you beat this poor river to a
froth, and I would imagine you heard about all your shortcom-
ings from my partner. I know you didn't stagger in til eleven-
fifteen, and David had to bang on the door of the restaurant to
get you supper. So I figure here we are, the last day of your trip,
and on the best river in the West, which shows excellent planning, and I thought maybe you'd like to fish civilized for a
change, instead of all obsessive and neurotic, which comes
more natural to you."

He waved his hand at the gobbling trout. "Room for one
man to cast. Room for the other two of us to spectate, tell
tales, sip coffee. Kibitz. Mock and deride the angler, should the
occasion present itself. Which I guarantee it will."

"You mean," said Andy slowly, "only one of us will fish at a
time?"

Bill turned to me. "Doctor Gill, here, obviously didn't completely squander his youth at medical school. He can still draw
a shrewd inference when he puts his mind to it. Yes, sir. One at
a time. Like gentlemen."

"One at a time," muttered Andy.

"I like it," I said. "I can watch you fish, pick up a few point-
ers. Want to flip for it?"

Andy shrugged. He snaked his hand down inside his waders
and came up with a quarter. He flipped it into the air. "Call
it," he said.

37

"Tails."

He caught the coin, slapped it on his wrist, glanced at it, and shoved it back into his pocket. "Heads," he said, and was out of the boat and into the water before I could lodge a protest.

He waded into a shallow slickwater, a cushion inside the heavier currents that carried fish food against the face of a steep cliff. It was one of those rivers-within-the-river characteristic of the Bighorn, whose currents braid and intersect and rub against one another with infinite complexity. It was a natural funnel, literally scummed over with dead and living insects and bits of weeds. It churned with feeding trout.

They ate with economical greed. No splashes or boils, no smashing tails against the water. Just heads lifting rhythmically to suck in what came their way. Dozens and dozens of heads. We could actually hear them slurp and slobber. Bighorn trout sustain themselves on tiny insects, and they seem to realize that if they expend much energy in eating any one of them, they will use up more calories than they consume. So they simply lie in the current and tilt up to feed. They prefer gentle flows to the heavier midriver currents for the same reasons. Especially the larger trout.

"Don't go flock shooting, now," said Bill.

Within ten minutes, one of those snouts sucked in Andy's self-tied #18 Pale Morning Dun imitation, and after a couple of reel-screeching runs Andy hand-landed a fat, red-spotted, eighteen-inch Bighorn brown.

"Nice, average fish," shrugged our guide.

Fifteen minutes, one break-off, and several missed strikes later I managed to land a twin of Andy's fish. Our pod of trout continued to gorge unabated.

As we watched Andy wade out for his turn, Bill turned to me. "I keep telling you," he said, "Best dry-fly fishing for trout in the world."

"Unfortunately," I said, "I haven't fished the world. Yet. But I can't imagine anything better."

The Bighorn River at least makes an excellent case for itself as the best fly-fishing river in the West, which probably makes it the best in the lower forty-eight. I still haven't fished them all, though I'm working on it. But the Bighorn remains the benchmark by which I measure all the others I know. So far, none has quite measured up.

Electroshock samples conducted by the Montana Department of Fish, Wildlife and Parks in a 7.2-mile stretch of the upper river between the Afterbay Dam and the Bighorn fishing access in September, 1986, found an estimated 7,031 one-year and older brown trout per mile of river, of which 576 were eighteen inches or longer. The same study counted 740 rainbows per mile, of which 238 were at least eighteen inches. That figures out to be one and a half catchable trout per surface foot of river. Local guides assert confidently, and my own experience confirms it, that the sizes and numbers have improved since then.

A similar study conducted on some of the most famous Montana rivers several years earlier concluded that the Bighorn boasted nearly twice as many twenty-inch trout per mile as the Beaverhead, which is considered by many to be the best trophy trout river in the West. No other river was even close.

What makes the case for the Bighorn as the best is its character, as much as its dense trout population. Its relatively constant water temperatures, typical of tailwater fisheries, guarantee a long growth period for trout and, combined with its high alkalinity, encourage prolific insect reproduction. Because the Bighorn does not produce sculpins and other big-trout forage the way freestone rivers do, its trout, even the large ones, key on insect hatches—to the fly caster's delight.

For the fisherman's convenience, it seems, the Bighorn, despite its great volume of water, is relatively slow moving, with plenty of bars, riffles, side channels, pools, and slicks to explore. It's easy to wade and stalk the Bighorn for feeding fish, and it offers the angler a seemingly limitless variety of types of water to cast to. However, finding pods of large trout such as Andy and I have fished to with Bill Rohrbacher and his partner, David Schuller, requires both the expertise of experienced guides like Bill and Dave plus the mobility of a boat. There are only three public accesses in the upper Bighorn. The river flows through a Crow Indian reservation, and walking to the river across that land is forbidden.

The Bighorn is still a young river. Before 1965 it ran slow, silty, and warm. When the Yellowtail Dam was built, it began to acquire tailwater characteristics. Browns flocked to it. Then in 1975 the Crows closed it, and it wasn't reopened until 1981, by Supreme Court edict. Fish biologists have electroshocked the river every year since then. In spite of growing fishing pressure and a couple summers of low water, the numbers of brown trout have increased consistently, which is attributable to ideal water temperatures for the fall spawners plus the steadily improving general quality of the water.

Until very recently, efforts to establish rainbows in the Bighorn appeared only marginally successful. They have been planted in varying numbers since 1966, most recently in 1983, but they did not seem to establish themselves the way browns have. One reason may be that rainbows have been caught—and kept—in greater numbers by bait fishermen and spin casters. Also, the Bighorn offers rainbows fewer suitable spawning grounds, and, as spring spawners, rainbows reproduce when the water is coldest and least nurturing for fry.

Beginning in 1988, however, the Bighorn introduced a no-kill regulation for rainbows, which, evidently, has made all the difference. Whereas during our two-day 1987 trip Andy and I caught exactly one rainbow (out of an estimated ninety trout), in two days in 1988 and three in 1989 we guessed that our rainbow-to-brown ratio was one to three. Several of our rainbows have been in the twenty-inch category, and we've busted off a few considerably larger. Dave Schuller predicts that in a few years the Bighorn will become one of the premier western rivers for trophy-sized rainbows.

Trout can be taken virtually year-round on the Bighorn. Streamers and nymphs work during all seasons, and the guides agree that an angler's best bet for taking a Bighorn trophy—something twenty-four inches or bigger—is on a Woolly Bugger or Matuka streamer.

It's a river that's accessible to novices as well as experts. Beginners can drift San Juan worms beneath a strike indicator over the bow of a driftboat and catch plenty of big trout. Accomplished nymph fishermen like Dave Schuller bounce tiny midge and mayfly-larva imitations through riffles and take some of the truly large trout of the river. Gary Borger, in his video of the river, proclaims the Bighorn the best nymph-fishing river in America. I think it's simply the best trout river in America.

For those inclined as Andy and I are, the Bighorn is, above all, a dry-fly river. We love to stalk the lineups of big trout heads that rise daintily in the slack water inside the main currents, often in less than a foot of water. We explore side channels, back-currents, and shallow flats. The larger Bighorn trout seem to seek out such places, away from heavy flows, where they find a lavish smorgasbord of bugs on which to gluttonize.

Andy and I have only fished the Bighorn during the summer months, but we are told it's good practically all year. A warm day in February often sparks a midge hatch, which will bring

41

big mixed pods of browns and rainbows working the surface. In March come dependable midge and *Baetis* hatches. From March through the end of May one can just about always find good dry-fly fishing on the Bighorn.

June through mid-July tends to be an off time for surface activity, but nymphs work consistently. Pale Morning Duns, yellow stoneflies, and Blue-Winged Olives arrive in the second or third week in July, heralding the real beginning of the dry-fly season on the Bighorn. The caddis get going in August, bringing in midmonth some truly incredible evening hatches of black caddis, which the guides feel is the most exciting hatch of the year. All this lasts well into October. Many locals believe that September and October is the best time of all to fish the Bighorn.

Rarely did fifteen minutes pass without a fish being caught. The trout seemed to run to a size—sixteen to eighteen inches—which Bill said was typical. "There are trout everywhere," he said. "They seem to school up in size categories. You want to catch a million twelve-inchers, you can do that, standing in one spot. You want to hunt for a real trophy, you can do that too, though those fish tend to be loners. Guys like Dave and I, we know the river, we can find you what you want."

It was fast fishing, but not easy. After a couple hours at that pod of trout, a lull arrived. The fish continued to feed, but they spurned our offerings. "Time to look for more fish?" I said.

Bill smiled at me and held up one finger. "Rule number one," he said. "Never leave rising fish."

I nodded.

"Rule number two," he added. "Never violate rule number one."

Bill bent over and stuck his face close to the surface, squinted, then straightened and grinned triumphantly. "They've switched to *Baetis* spinners," he proclaimed.

A few hours later, they switched back to Pale Morning Duns. Their gorging never stopped. We never moved.

His advice to avoid flock-shooting proved sound. Six or eight trout might be munching regularly within a circle six feet in diameter. We usually found ourselves casting tiny flies on 6X tippets, impossible for our eyes to distinguish from the real stuff littering the water. The trout didn't need to move to find plenty to eat. A blind cast into the middle of the pod would float through feeding trout, and the angler would have no idea if any of those black noses were sucking in his fly. Striking randomly only spooked the fish. Andy and I learned to pick a single fish and cast only to him, finding his rhythm and laying the leader tippet directly between his eyes. If he lifted his snout at the right time, odds were that he was sipping in the invisible fly at the end of our leader. "You've got to make your best guess," advised Bill. "When in doubt, set that hook. No guts, no glory."

Afternoon stretched into evening. Andy and I continued to take turns. We still hadn't moved. Finally, after Andy netted one more ho-hum eighteen-incher, Bill said, "We've got many miles to row to the takeout. One more fish, okay?"

I waded out and Bill came with me. He pointed to a snout. "Try that one."

I dropped my fly three feet directly upstream of his dimple. His toad-shaped nose lifted and he sucked in the tiny fly. I set the hook and he took off. This would be the thirty-sixth trout Andy and I took from that single pod that day. An even three dozen. It figured to more than three trout, averaging seventeen inches, on dry flies, per man hour. I turned downstream to play him.

"Look," whispered Bill. "Look at that."

A rainbow bisected the darkening eastern horizon. It seemed to touch earth in the middle of the river, where my trout leaped, glistening in the last golden rays of the setting sun. "Pot 'o gold," said Bill. "Beautiful."

OUT OF THE FRYING PAN

We were bumping up through the narrow valley, three neo-prened six-footers crammed into the front seat of Sandy Moore's pickup. Red rock outcroppings towered above us on the left, glowing in the angled morning sunlight. Golden October aspen stands dribbled down the steep hillsides on both sides of the road, mixing and mingling with blue-green patches of evergreen. The winding road followed the river, which churned and twisted through its boulder-strewn channel on our right.

It looked like a typical mountain stream. I've seen dozens just like it in Vermont. You'd need no double haul to cast from one bank to the other. It looked as if a man in hip boots could cross it in most places without getting his pants wet.

The Frying Pan. Andy and I had come from Massachusetts to this little place near Aspen, Colorado, for the long Columbus Day weekend with one thing in mind.

The farther up toward the headwaters of the river we traveled, the more cars we saw stopped beside the road. Every pool seemed to have two or three people standing in it. I couldn't decide whether this was a good sign or a bad one.

45

As we rode, Sandy talked about his river. His delivery was soft, understated. Often he'd pause and jerk his head at the river. "Big guy lives there, against that flat boulder."

"How big?"

Shrug. "No one's been able to land him yet. Several've hooked him."

"Like *how big*?"

"Big. One of the big ones."

Later. "See where the river funnels between those two rocks? Mean Joe Green's residence. We can try for him later."

"How big is Mean Joe Green?"

"Mean Joe? Oh, he's really big."

Big. That's what we had come here for.

Back in March, when we were organizing our fishing year and Andy asked me what I wanted to do in October, that was my answer. "Big. I want to catch a big trout on a light fly rod with a small fly in a river."

Andy's question later became the familiar one. "How big is big?" he said.

When I was a kid, anything longer than the hatchery ten-inch norm was big. A foot was a bragging trout. My big-trout standard went up in small increments, perhaps an inch for every ten years of my life. In my New England trout streams, a fourteen-incher is a "nice fish." We call a sixteen-incher a monster, as in "monster brown." I've caught very few monster browns in New England. It was never really the point. We fish for the trout that are there. A trout is a trout in New England, and we're happy with all of them.

When Andy and I started going out West, my standards got confused. Corrupted, some would say. I learned to yawn at fourteen-inchers. Seventeen inches became a sort of norm. I've caught plenty of eighteen-, nineteen-, twenty-inchers. Once

46

any one of those would have been the fish of a lifetime. Now I can recall only a few of them, caught under unusual circumstances.

Now, anything longer than twenty inches is big.

I busted off a gulping brown on Hebgen Lake that Bob Lamm, our guide, opined would've measured twenty-six inches. A rainbow that ate my Woolly Bugger in the Box Canyon straightened the hook. Those two trout were big. But I didn't catch them.

"I want to catch a trout that you measure in pounds, not inches," I told Andy. "I mean *big.*"

We had heard about the Frying Pan. We heard it was a lot like New Zealand. Sight fishing for big trout with nymphs and dry flies. Yeah, but how big? It was hard to pin anybody down. We decided to try it.

And now we were there.

The river was not, frankly, impressive. Pretty, but otherwise disappointing to look at. It was hard to imagine big trout living in it.

"There," said Sandy. "See him?"

We were standing on the rocky bank. He was pointing at a place a little upstream from us, where a riffle dropped into a narrow run.

I looked. "No," I said. "I don't see anything."

He took my fly rod and pointed with it. "You can see his side."

I squinted along the nine feet of thin graphite. "Yeah," I said. "I think so." I saw a red swatch of color hovering above the gravelly bottom. It was a very large swatch of color. I tried to imagine the rainbow trout whose side was broad enough to carry all that color on it.

"Okay," he said. "Here's the drill. Short line. Pinpoint casts. You've got to drift it right into his mouth. These fat piggies don't like to move far to eat. The river's full of junk for them. Keep a straight line. Follow it downstream with your rod. When your strike indicators pass over him, be ready. Don't wait to see the indicators move. That's too late. You won't see the fish move, either. They suck in and spit out these little nymphs in a second. You have to sense the take. Got it?"

"I guess so," I said. I always get nervous, performing in front of experts, especially guides, who gauge their own success by that of their clients and seem to take it personally when their clients fail, which I have a habit of doing.

I checked the rig that Sandy had arranged. He had tied a #16 Hare's Ear Nymph to a twelve-foot knotless leader tapered to 4X. To the eye of the Hare's Ear Sandy had knotted a two-foot length of 6X. On the end of that tippet he had tied a #22 midge nymph, a simple little thing with a Flashabou body and a couple turns of peacock herl at the eye. He had wrapped one lead twist-on above the Hare's Ear. At the butt end of the leader Sandy had stuck on three pink strike indicators at six-inch intervals.

I plunked it six feet directly upstream of the crimson gash. "Yeah, good," Sandy whispered.

I followed the rig downstream with my rod. "There!" said Sandy.

"Huh?"

He looked at me and shook his head. "He took it."

"How could you tell?"

"You gotta sense it." He shrugged. "Let's go find another one."

48

It wasn't hard. Sandy had an eye for them, and after a while I got so I could see them, once he pointed them out. The river bottom seemed paved with trout. The game was to look for the big ones.

It was hard to judge their size underwater. I still didn't know what big was here.

I spooked one by dropping the twist-on on top of him. Another ignored repeated offerings. A third mouthed my nymph, according to Sandy. I failed to detect it. I was growing increasingly nervous, although Sandy seemed more tolerant than I deserved.

Fishing to one more greenish shape with a faint reddish blot, for some reason my rod hand twitched of its own accord, setting the hook into the corner of the trout's mouth. My rod bowed. The fish throbbed for a moment. I could feel his head thrashing in what seemed like mild irritation. Suddenly he crashed across the narrow pool, heading for a cluster of rocks. I hastily reeled in my slack. "Point your rod butt at him," said Sandy. "Be gentle. That's 6X."

Five minutes later Sandy netted him. The trout was shaped like a rugby ball. Sandy weighed the net with the fish in it. "Four and a half pounds," he said matter-of-factly.

"Minus how much for the net?"

"I calibrated this scale for the net. That's what the fish weighs."

Sandy measured him. He was eighteen and a half inches long. This was a trout to be measured in pounds. It was a big trout. It just didn't look much like any trout I'd ever seen.

Sandy wandered downstream to see how Andy was doing. I edged upstream, peering into the river. Now my eyes were trained and I could spot the trout, and gradually I withdrew into a kind of Zen state that tuned me in to the tiny hesitations in the leader, the little tap that vibrated in my fingers, and my hand, separate from my brain, began to hook trout.

By lunchtime I had landed half a dozen and lost at least that many. They were fat fish. No. They were gross and flabby. When I held one in my hand, his body seemed to sag, and my fingers sank into his flesh. Sandy weighed one that measured a hair less than seventeen inches. Three and a half pounds.

Were these big trout? Or were they just freaks? I couldn't decide.

Sandy set up folding chairs beside the stream for lunch. Andy gobbled his sandwiches and stepped into the river. Sandy and I watched his fish.

"Mysis shrimp," said Sandy.

"Huh?"

"I assume you were wondering how these trout got so fat. It's the mysis shrimp. After they built the dam, they stocked it with salmon. Then they introduced the shrimp for the salmon to eat. Except the shrimp went to the bottom, and the salmon didn't, so the shrimp had no predators and they multiplied extravagantly. And when they retrofitted the dam five or six years ago for hydroelectric, the turbines started to churn live shrimp into the river. See, after they built the dam, oh about twenty-five years ago, this turned into a pretty good trout stream. Lots of one-, two-pounders. About two hundred pounds of trout per acre, they figured, which is nice. But when those shrimp started spewing into the river, the trout just went absolutely bananas. They began to find lots of dead trout—gross, fat things. The biologists figured out they died from overeating. Literally. When they electroshocked the river, they found 975 pounds of trout per acre. I mean, that's unbelievable. Six-, eight-, ten-pound trout shaped like pregnant largemouth bass with little trout heads stuck on the end. There were times back in the first couple years of the shrimp when after a while clients'd bust off five-pounders so they could go after big ones."

"What's the biggest one you've seen?" I said.

Sandy grinned. "You're really into bigness, aren't you?"

I shrugged. "Just curious."

"I had a client catch one a little over thirteen pounds a couple years ago. Thirty inches. On a 5X tippet. I caught a nine-and-a-half-pounder last March." He waved his hand, as if these were not outrageous stories. "After the first couple years, the fish seemed to adapt to the shrimp, things stabilized, and they stopped dying. They just got fat. Hey!"

Andy had a fish. We watched him play it. He held his rod high. His reel zinged. "That's one of the streamlined ones," said Sandy. "Those fat ones, maybe you noticed, they're a little sluggish."

Andy's fish was an even four pounds, nineteen inches. Fatter than any New England trout, but healthy and solid. Sleek compared to most we'd been taking.

That evening Andy and I went to the Toilet Bowl, the deep pool immediately below the Reudi Dam where the turbines feed the river with cold shrimp-infested water from the bottom of the reservoir. We drifted #16 shrimp patterns through the deep currents, a different sort of fishing, more like using bait than flies, actually.

Just as the sun fell behind the mountains my wrist twitched at one of those imperceptible pauses in the leader. "Bottom," I announced when I raised my rod. Solid. I tried to jerk the fly loose. Then the bottom began to move, and I realized I was

51

tied to a big fish. Big! He moved away from me, across the pool, as slow and unconcerned and unswervable as a truck in low gear. I once foul-hooked a snapping turtle two feet across that acted the same way. I held my rod high. My reel clicked, also in low gear. Then the leader parted.

I reeled in. "That," I said to Andy, "was a big one. I wish I could have seen him."

For three days we caught football trout on tiny nymphs and 6X tippets. We learned to spot fish lying in the currents and estimate their sizes. We stalked them with care, we constantly adjusted the amount of lead we twisted onto our leaders, we entered at will into that abstract meditative state that put our subconscious senses in charge of detecting strikes. Andy busted off a rainbow he swore was twice as big as the four-pounder he'd caught. On two of those days in the early afternoon a hatch of Blue-Winged Olives came off, and we had fast fishing for eastern-standard rainbows on dry flies.

I was dissatisfied. I kept thinking about the snapping-turtle trout in the Toilet Bowl. My standards were as distorted as these Frying Pan rainbows. I wanted to catch one of the big ones.

When it happened, it seemed almost anticlimactic. Back in the Toilet Bowl, our last evening on the river. Another subtle twitch and mindless strike. Another snapping turtle. He didn't run, he didn't jump, he didn't thrash around. He was simply immovable. He swam in circles around the pool until he tired himself out, which took no more than ten minutes.

Andy netted him. He hooked his DeLiar onto his net with the fish in it. The scale clanked down to the bottom, its maximum. Eight pounds. The fish probably weighed nine. Maybe ten. We won't know. It was twenty-three and three-quarter inches long. It had the depth and the broad shoulders of a tuna. We photographed it, revived it, and released it. I felt vaguely let down, almost depressed. I can't explain it. It was by double the biggest trout of my life. I had caught the second biggest two days earlier.

The next morning we got up early and hightailed it for the Toilet Bowl. Andy's eyes blazed. He was determined.

I left my rod in the car. I'd caught my big trout.

While he was stringing his rod I spotted a good one feeding in the tail-out of the pool. Andy waded in and nailed him. Five and a half pounds. I got several good pictures.

We still had an hour. We drove down to the pool where Andy had broken off the big one on our second day. I toted my camera halfway up the hill to shoot some scenery. Andy was a tiny red-shirted spot far down in the silver ribbon of the stream. His shout echoed up to me. I stumbled down the hill. By the time I got there, he was netting the fish.

It, too, clanked his DeLiar to the bottom.

I took pictures. He released his trout and reeled in. "Let's get out of here," he said. "We've got a plane to catch."

Some day, when the urge to catch a really big trout overwhelms me, I expect I'll go back to the Frying Pan. March, they say, is a good month. The rainbows are spawning. But December is good, too. That's when the browns spawn. There aren't the crowds then, either.

Some day. But probably not soon.

THE GIANT TARPON
OF BELIZE

"I had thees dream last night," our guide Pancho told us on the morning of our fourth day in Belize. "I hooked a giant tarpon, and when he leaped, he leaped so high he hung heemself in the mangrove trees. I could not get heem down."

"What happened?" I said.

Pancho shrugged. "I woke up. I got out of bed, I brushed my teeth. Then I looked at my watch. It was two-thirty. I went back to bed."

"The wind," I said. "Was the wind blowing in your dream?"

He nodded. "Always the wind."

We discussed Pancho's dream. We tried to make an omen of it. It was difficult. The flats seemed so vast. And so empty. And so windy.

That persistent, cursed wind chopped at the surface of the flats off Cangrejo Cay, as it had for all the previous days. Lousy tarpon conditions. The wind muddied the water. It put the fish off their feed, drove them from the flats, ruined the fisherman's visibility.

I squinted through the glare of the high equatorial sun, telling myself to concentrate, to search for anomalies—greenish ghostlike shapes that would be cruising tarpon. From my perch on the casting platform in the bow of Pancho's twenty-two-foot flat-bottomed fiberglass skiff, I rocked on the corrugated sea.

Belize is about the size of Vermont, and less populated. It snuggles peacefully between Mexico and Guatemala, untouched by the political turmoil of its neighbors. Commercial fishing and, only recently, tourism are its main industries. The ruins of an ancient Mayan civilization have been discovered deep in the jungles of Belize. Anthropologists and other curious folk brave the humid heat to visit them. A barrier reef—the second largest barrier reef in the world—extends the entire length of the country. Most of its natives—Mexicans and Mayan Indians—speak and understand English.

Inside the reef lie vast flats studded with islands (called cays) where hoards of fly-rod targets swim—bonefish, tarpon, permit, barracuda, jack crevalle, snapper, and ladyfish. The water is normally flat and clear. It's ideal for fly fishing and scuba diving. Most of Belize's tourists are interested in one of those sports or the other.

I knew none of this when Mike Lawson, the guru of the Henry's Fork, called me in January. "I'm organizing a trip to Belize," he said. I didn't tell him I had never heard of Belize. "The fishing for bonefish and tarpon is pretty good there," he added in his typically understated manner.

"Pretty good," he admitted when I pressed him, meant catching a dozen bones off the mangrove flats in a morning. It meant that in Belize one might have a legitimate shot at hooking a permit on a fly.

What perked up my ears, though, were his tales of sighting a hundred tarpon a day, of "jumping" six or eight of them, and of landing a couple. This, Mike said, had happened to him every day of the week he had spent there the previous April. April, May, and June were prime months for tarpon. Oh, yes, and these were the giant tarpon, seventy, eighty, one hundred pounds. "Kinda fun on a fly rod," drawled Mike.

The tarpon flats in the vicinity of Ambergris Cay, where we would be staying, are generally conceded to offer the best fishing of its kind in Central and South America, he added. Mike Lawson is very cautious about using the word "best."

I had read Lefty Kreh and Ted Williams on the subject. I believed that catching a giant tarpon on a fly was the ultimate angling thrill.

Andy and I discussed it. For all of five minutes. We told Mike to count us in. Then I looked up Belize in my atlas.

For three and a half days Andy and I swapped one-hour shifts on the platform. We carefully stripped eighty feet of 12-weight fly line into neat, tangleproof (we hoped) coils, and stood, poised with our powerful fly rods, dangling the gaudy streamers we had tied back in February. Pancho poled us slowly across the flats of Savannah and Mosquito and Cangrejo. Sometimes, in places that looked to me like all the other miles of flats, Pancho would ram his pole into the bottom, three or four feet beneath the surface, snub the stern line to it, and we would sit stationary.

And we would stare into the empty sea. And wait.

On Tuesday we had seen tarpon. "Feesh!" said Pancho in a loud, excited whisper. "Tarpons!" I looked wildly about.

"There! I see them!" said Andy. "Three o'clock."

Then I spotted them, too, blurry pale green shapes cruising up from behind us. I false-cast once, tried to shoot line. All that practicing, and when it counted my timing deserted me. My fly fell short.

"Again! Queek!" yelled Pancho, no whisper this time.

Too late again. The shapes had dematerialized.

Pancho shook his head. "You got to see heem queek," he said. "You got to show heem the fly."

Every tarpon fisherman, I told myself, had to be a novice at one time. It was small consolation.

Later that afternoon Pancho spotted another pod when Andy was in the bow. As suddenly as they had appeared, they evaporated beyond casting range.

And those two moments of excitement had to sustain us through the empty hours. It required a superhuman effort of imagination to translate the unreality of those wraithlike images into the truth of all we had read and been told. Other people's stories are abstractions. You believe them, men like Lefty Kreh and Ted Williams. But their tales hold no reality for one who has never experienced them.

It took us two hours to fly from Miami to Belize City on TACA Airlines. There Andy and I and three scuba divers crammed ourselves and our gear into a single-engine five-seater, the pride of Maya Air, for the half-hour flight over the vast flats dotted with jungly, uninhabited cays. We landed on the dirt strip in the sleepy fishing village of San Pedro on Ambergris Cay. There we were met by Pancho, who would be our guide for the week. We piled our stuff into his boat and he motored us through three miles of narrow mangrove-lined cuts in the island

57

to El Pescador, the small resort where we would stay for the week.

"Meet me at seex-thirty," said Pancho. "We catch some bones, then we go after the tarpons."

In the mornings, on the rising tides, Pancho poled us along the shallow mangrove flats where we stalked schools of bonefish. Sometimes we could spot their tails waving in the air as they nosed the soft coral bottom for shrimp. Sometimes all we could see was the "nervous water" their movements made.

It took me a while to recognize nervous water. Pancho always saw it first.

There seemed to be unlimited bonefish. They didn't run large, by bonefish standards. Two to four pounds. But they lived up to their reputations. Hundred-yard nonstop reel-screaming runs.

We cast—without success—to permit. We caught a lemon shark and a Spanish mackerel.

After supper in the dining room the fly fishermen shared stories. Everyone was nailing the bones. One party had taken some 'cuda on spinning outfits. Someone had induced a permit to strike his crab fly. Mike and his son, Shaun, doubled on jacks.

Always, inevitably, the conversation turned to the wind. Bad for tarpon. Everyone wanted tarpon. A few had been spotted. Nobody had jumped one.

We had all come here to catch a giant tarpon.

After three and a half days, I began to realize that it was entirely possible—perhaps even probable—that the week could pass without ever getting a shot at a tarpon. This truth usually got left out of tarpon-fishing literature, and even though I recognized it also as a truth of life, it was hard to accept it philosophically. We had come so far. It had cost so much. We deserved a tarpon.

I stood there in the bow, rocking and staring. And I recognized what it was about tarpon fishing that Lefty and Ted and the others rarely tell. The same thing applies to big-game fishing and hunting of all kinds—and to a great deal of small-game sport as well.

A man I know, an electrician named Frank, spends his only week of vacation every summer stalking Atlantic salmon in the Narraguagus River in Maine. He's been doing this for twenty-three years. He has yet to land a salmon. I keep asking him why he doesn't choose a more rewarding sport. He just shrugs. "You want big rewards, you've got to make big investments," he says.

Another friend of mine, a newcomer to big-game fly fishing, landed a big salmon from the President's Pool of the Penobscot River on the first morning of his first day of salmon fishing. I hesitated to tell Frank about it. I figured he'd curse beginner's luck, and his own. But he simply smiled. "Your friend got gypped," he said.

I have dragged streamer flies around Maine landlocked salmon lakes for three-day weekends without a single strike. I have plodded through miles of New Hampshire juniper and blowdown without flushing a grouse. I have seen Vermont's storied Battenkill appear as barren of trout as the morning puddles in my driveway.

In these cases, memories have sustained me. I find it easy to stay interested. I just conjure up mental images—the throbbing in my wrist of a running salmon, or the sound of an exploding grouse, or the picture of the sipping rise of a large brown trout.

59

Memories keep me going: The next pass by a rocky point will bring a strike, the next apple and pine corner will hold a brood of grouse, the next pool will show a feeding trout. It's happened too many times. It will happen again.

But out there on Cangrejo I had no memories. Just secondhand stories. And none of those tales had prepared me for the empty days. I remembered Frank's words. But there was never a guarantee that an investment would pay off. It was hard to keep the faith.

I marveled at the many shades of green and blue painted over the vast tarpon flats inside the barrier reef. I watched the frigate birds and the pelicans chase needlefish and mullets. I practiced double-hauling. And when Andy was in the bow I resharpened hooks and tied up more terminal rigs with my newly learned Bimini Twist and Albright knot and Homer Rhodes Loop knot. I thought about the shower and the ceremonial pull on our jug of Rebel Yell and the siesta after Pancho dropped us off at El Pescador, the fresh snapper and the deep-fried conch and the exotic tropical vegetables at dinner, the fishing talk over coffee, the early bedtime for the sun-beaten angler far from taxicab and telephone. And I knew that all these were important parts of tarpon fishing.

I stared into the water. I shifted the heavy rod from hand to hand.

"Feesh!"

I turned. Pancho was pointing to the right. I saw them. Six or seven green, almost translucent wraiths. I pivoted and threw an awkward crosshand cast at them. It came up short. I lifted the line. Miraculously, the school turned. They were crossing our bow. Sixty, seventy feet out. Double haul forgotten, I heaved the fly. Short again.

"Streep! Streep!" yelled Pancho.

I stripped. A shape peeled away from the school. He followed, followed, followed—and the gaudy streamer disappeared. An instinct heaved back on my heavy rod. And from the water climbed a tarpon, rising straight up like a Poseidon missile. Great head thrashing, silver body arched, my self-tied fly an orange speck in the corner of his huge mouth, he rainbowed high against the tropical sky and crashed into the water. Instinctively I had "bowed" to him, depriving the great fish of taut line to fall upon.

"Heet heem again!" yelled Pancho. I jabbed hard, three times, attempting to drive the hook solidly into the big tarpon's concrete mouth.

Line zizzed from my reel. He turned, angling toward us. I reeled. Then another leap. And another. Six leaps in all, one after the other, all within one hundred feet of the skiff, all within two or three minutes.

"A beeg one," observed Pancho, calm now. "Seex feet, maybe. Eighty, ninety pounds."

The giant fish circled the boat three times, pausing twice to roll to the surface. Then he was off and running. It was not the screeching flight of a bonefish, but it was irresistible, and I could only tighten the drag and watch the line peel away and the backing diminish. Once, far far out on the flat he leaped again, as high as ever, a silvery shape arched over the dark green of the mangroves of Cangrejo Cay. It looked as if he would descend into the jungle. Pancho's dream.

I could feel him slog, his great muscles writhing and twisting, his head shaking slowly back and forth. With pressure from my powerful rod, I would gain a few feet of line. Moments later he would take it back.

As I stood in Pancho's skiff with cramped arms and rod

butt jammed painfully into my stomach, I recognized that there was another truth to tarpon fishing, a corollary to Frank's philosophy: The reward fully justifies the investment. Days of boredom, aching muscles, red burning eyes—they are costs that *ought* to be risked for such a valuable payoff. I was tied to the fish of a lifetime, separated by 150 yards of backing, fly line, and leader, including two feet of slender 15-pound Maxima.

I was glad, then, that it hadn't happened too soon.

It settled into a battle of muscle and will, and I had no certainty that I possessed more of either than did that magnificent tarpon. I began to understand for the first time the mystical link between Hemingway's Old Man and his fish.

If I catch you, great fish, I will jump into the water with you and hold you in my arms. I want to be photographed hugging you. Then I will release you. Don't resist me, fish. I am your friend. I tied this fly you have eaten one snowy New England Sunday afternoon months ago. I have tried to imagine you from stories other men have told. But I couldn't imagine you. You are bigger and stronger and more noble than I ever could have known.

The backing sagged far out over the flat. I could not see where it linked with the line. Still I could feel the pulse of my fish.

I hung on.

There was no sudden surge, no desperate leap, no warning. And no life at the end of my line. I reeled in.

I lifted the fly from the water. I looked at Andy. "Aw," he said. "Aw, nuts." He checked his watch. "Forty-five minutes. You had him on forty-five minutes."

Pancho grinned and shook his head. "Nine out of ten tarpons get away," he said. "The hook pulls out. It wears a hole in hees mouth. Nothing you can do about it. You did good."

Nine out of ten get away. Another truth about tarpon fishing. And life.

I stared out over the Cangrejo flats, as vast and empty as ever, yet now transformed into a new beauty. For me, the hook of the tarpon would never pull out.

Part 3
THE FLY FETISH

When Andy and I travel, as we do several times a year now in our Sisyphean quest to cast flies to trout in every river in the world, we spend our evenings tying flies. Invariably, the flies we fashion are designed to catch yesterday's trout, those that spurned all the offerings from the dozens of boxes that bulge from our vests.

Last evening's creations rarely work on tomorrow's trout.

We find they're too big. Or too small. Or the bodies are the wrong shade of olive. Or too fat. Or too thin. Or we ought to have tied emergers, or crippled duns, or spinners that haven't yet turned rusty. Or we should've done Parachutes, or No-Hackles, or Comparaduns. *Baetis*, or *inermis*, or *Callibaetis*.

I never know exactly what's wrong with my flies. But I believe something is, because they never work as well as I think they should. I persist in my faith that the right fly at the right time will enable me to catch trout regularly and effortlessly.

Part of me recognizes that much of this is esoteric nonsense, and that if it happened that way something would be wrong anyway. Catching fish on flies isn't supposed to happen regularly and effortlessly. It's the irregularity and the effortfulness of it that makes it special. And I know that there are countless other variables besides fly pattern that factor into an angler's success, that guarantee it will always be difficult and unpredictable. Many of these variables are associated with the angler's skills and techniques. Mine, for sure, are imperfect, and always will be.

That's why I continue to focus on the fly. It's one variable I can control.

I have, belatedly, learned to don the cheaters I now must use for reading the newspaper and tying improved clinch knots. I bend my face to within inches of the river's surface. The messages I read there are usually fascinating, but inconclusive. In my eastern trout streams, I often fail to detect anything at all that looks like fish food. Yet the trout are feeding. And in the fertile tailwater rivers and spring creeks of the West, I invariably discover lavish fish buffets floating on the currents. Spinners and duns of several mayfly species, midges in varying stages of hatching, a bewildering assortment of terrestrials, caddis, stoneflies, all drift past my myopic scrutiny. And none of that takes into account what's going on beneath the surface.

I see the trout eating. I understand that sometimes they dine selectively, sometimes opportunistically. Already I have tried all the logical things. I have failed to interest more than the oddball trout. If only I had the right fly . . .

Andy calls it "pattern anxiety." The fly fisherman so afflicted is easily diagnosed. He stands midstream, his rod tucked under his arm, his head bent to his open fly box. He pokes around, plucks a fly from his box, holds it to the light, frowns, returns it, pokes around some more. Finally he shifts, and we see him aiming a leader tippet into the eye of a hook. He grunts, curses, tries again. He dampens his knot in his mouth, pulls it tight, nips off the tail of tippet. He squeezes a worm of Gink onto his fingers, strokes his fly, false-casts. He drops his fresh fly above a rising trout. Once, twice, three times. He strips in his line. He tucks his rod under his arm and removes another fly box from another pocket of his vest.

And so on.

I fantasize about the perfect fly. Sometimes I persuade myself that it actually exists. On occasion, even, I have believed I have discovered it. I imagine carrying but one fly box, filled with that single, magic pattern. I will tie one on and keep fishing until the trout chew it up. Then I'll tie on a fresh one. Simple. Deadly. I will concentrate on my technique, certain in my knowledge that at least I've got the right thing tied to my tippet. I will discover the final antidote for pattern anxiety and take my rightful place alongside the great healers of our civilization.

Alas. I can't even cure myself.

BEETLES AT HIGH NOON

If some joker in the Fish and Wildlife office decreed that trout anglers could only fish with one size of a single fly pattern, I would not feel particularly handicapped.

I wouldn't like it. But I could live with it.

I'd simply fill a fly box with #14 black deerhair beetles, confident that I'd hold my own with even my more skilled counterparts on just about any trout stream in the country.

Actually, I've done it, although by choice and not coercion.

And it's worked. Not always. But often.

Bob Lamm, by consensus the best guide in the West Yellowstone area, showed me that the beetle is more than just another terrestrial imitation one morning on the fabled Railroad Ranch stretch of the Henry's Fork. I waded beside him through the frigid hip-deep water trying to match his skill at estimating the sizes of the trout snouts that lifted here and there to suck in the tiny Trico spinners that blanketed the surface.

"There's a good one," he said, pointing. It looked like all the rest to me, but I knew better than to question Bob's judgment. He gestured to my rod. "What've you got tied on there?"

I showed him my fake #20 black-and-white spinner. He shrugged. "Try it," he said.

On the Ranch, you cast across and down to the finicky trout, then shake out some slack to extend the float. I did it rather well, for me. But that particular rainbow ignored my offering. After half a dozen tries, Bob said, "Gimme that thing."

He clipped off my fly, fumbled in his vest, and came out with something big and black and buggy. He proceeded to thread it onto my tippet.

"A beetle?" I said. "You kidding?"

"Nope. He'll eat it."

I cast it as before, and when it floated over that trout, a nose the size of a garden toad appeared in its path and the beetle disappeared. I was so startled that I forgot to strike.

But since then, I have always been prepared to strike. Because nothing that happens when I tie on a beetle surprises me.

Japanese beetles were first identified as trout forage on the Pennsylvania limestone creeks by Charles Fox and Vincent Marinaro in the early 1940s. It was Fox who fashioned the pioneer beetle "fly" by gluing a coffee bean to the stripped-down remnants of an old Light Cahill. Marinaro refined the imitation considerably by tying a large jungle-cock nail flat over a hook shank prewound with black hackle.

Both flies, by Marinaro's account, fooled the fussy trout of the Letort, and the beetle as a trout fly was born.

But the Letort masters generally restricted their use of the fake beetle to "hatch-matching" situations. Most anglers, including me, followed their lead and tied on a beetle imitation when we observed real beetles on the water, just as we employed ant or hopper or inchworm imitations to match those "hatches." These conditions happened rarely. Hence, I hardly ever used beetles. That is, until I met Bob Lamm.

Those big Henry's Fork rainbows are famed—and cursed—for their selectivity. Yet that morning, alternating between tiny imitations of the variety of mayflies that were hatching and bulky deerhair beetles, we figured we rose more to the beetle, which resembled nothing whatsoever that we could see on the water.

"I figure even these trout are suckers for a mouthful," opined Bob when I asked his theory. "They learn, if that's what you call it in pea-brained organisms like trout, that beetles are tasty and nourishing, and this gets imprinted in what passes for their minds." He shrugged. "Whatever. It works. And it actually seems to work better on big fish than small ones."

This has been my experience under many different conditions on trout rivers and streams from Massachusetts to Montana. Whenever trout are looking up, they are usually eager to eat beetles.

Last summer when Andy and I stalked the persnickety trout of Armstrong's and Depuy's spring creeks, we fished nothing but beetles all day long. In the morning, when Pale Morning Duns were hatching and the streams were pocked with the rings of feeding trout, we took them on beetles. During midday we drifted beetles tight against the streamside brush and logjams and had wonderful luck on sipping bank feeders. Through the afternoon doldrums, when nothing particular seemed to be on the surface, and through the later sulphur hatch and the evening midge emergences, we continued to fish beetles. And the action was continuous.

We didn't do this for the sake of experiment, or to handicap ourselves. We did it because we had learned that beetles work under all of these conditions.

Whether the trout are feeding selectively, opportunistically, or hardly at all, the beetle seems to hold an appeal that they can't resist. On the heavily pounded catch-and-release waters of such New England rivers as the Swift, Deerfield, and Farmington, the beetle has proved especially effective for me, perhaps because those fish have seen mock beetles less frequently than the more refined mayfly imitations most anglers employ.

Anyone with even the most rudimentary fly-tying equipment can fashion a season's supply of beetles in an evening. They are easy—and even fun—to make. Because creating the same fly repeatedly tends to bore me, I tie several different styles, although I can't say that I've found one that works better than the others.

I make most of my beetles on #14 hooks, a vast relief to these middle-aged eyes from the #20s typically required to match many of our hatches. I'll carry a few #16 beetles for those rare occasions I've run into when the trout seem to prefer something a bit more delicate.

I like to tie in a little bunch of white or neon-colored deer hair or globug yarn onto the back of the neck of my beetles. Trout, evidently, can't see what's on the sky side of floating flies. But fishermen can. A #14 black beetle is nearly invisible without that speck of color. With it, I have no trouble following the drift of my fly.

The black deerhair beetle is probably the easiest to make. Simply tie in the butt end of a small bunch of black deer hair behind the eye of the hook, wind over the deer hair down to the bend in the shank and then back to the eye, fold over the deer hair, and tie it down. Clip off the flared ends, leaving a little bulk for the head, and also leave a few straggling longer

71

ends for legs. Tie in a tiny bunch of bright-colored hair or yarn on top of the hook behind the head for visibility and clip it close. *Voilà.*

Beetles can also be fashioned like miniature deerhair bass bugs. Tie in two or three bunches of deer hair, allowing it to spin and flare around the shank of the hook. Then trim it to the shape of a beetle. Tie in half a dozen hairs under the thorax for legs. Add a tuft of color on top.

The Marinaro design also works well, although I find it to be the fussiest to make. First I wind the hook shank with a strand of peacock herl, which I then overwind with black hackle. I trim the hackle to open V's, top and bottom, and then tie in a black hackle tip (Marinaro's choice, a jungle-cock nail, is no longer available) flat over the top, and finish with a large head of black thread.

Polycelon, a synthetic material resembling dense foam rubber, makes beetles that fool trout as readily as those fashioned from natural materials. Polycelon beetles have the additional advantages of floating forever, and whereas trout teeth can quickly destroy the delicate deer-hair or feather imitations, the synthetic is virtually indestructible.

This version is tied similarly to the deerhair beetle. Cut a strip of Polycelon one inch by one-quarter inch, lay it on top of the hook shank, tie it down at the eye, wind back over the strip down to the bend and back to the eye, fold the strip over the top and tie down at the eye. Trim off the head and add a wind or two of black hackle for legs and a speck of bright-colored hair or yarn at the neck.

I've never tried to make a beetle out of a coffee bean.

Vince Marinaro, an astute observer of stream life, noted that live beetles rarely move or twitch when they float downstream.

Artificial beetles work best when fished with a dead, drag-free drift. A dragging beetle will put down a potential taker as quickly as a dragging mayfly imitation. I use fine tippets—usually 6X—to minimize the subtle effects of complex currents when fishing on smooth surfaces such as we find on western spring creeks. Even on heavier broken water, I rarely go coarser than 4X.

Then there are the exceptions. Last summer on Armstrong Spring Creek I located a good-sized trout sipping delicately a scant two inches from the edge of a logjam that projected into the stream. I could only approach him from upstream. My first several quartering-down casts passed within a foot of the log. That trout ignored them, but continued to feed, just the tip of his nose breaking the surface. My next try, I quickly realized, was on course to foul up on the log. As the beetle neared the feeding trout, I had to tug it away or else risk hanging up and losing my chance. The beetle dipped beneath the surface and I began to strip it back. Abruptly it stopped. It reappeared an instant later in the corner of the mouth of the fat brown trout that vaulted into the air. When he finally came to my net, he measured nineteen inches, my largest trout of that day. After that experience, when I have located a trout that seems uninterested in my beetle, I have sometimes found that a little twitch, or even a twitching subsurface retrieve, will cause the fish to change his mind.

For years I have been frustrated by the predictable early summer evening rise of trout in our eastern ponds. I'm certain that the trout are sipping midges too tiny to imitate. One evening while float-tubing I tied on a beetle. I tossed it toward the rings left by a bulging trout, let it sit, gave it a tiny twitch intended only to make the legs vibrate, and let it sit again.

A rainbow trout crashed it like a bass.

(Several subsequent trout, it must be noted, ignored the

same beetle. I can explain none of this. But I always find such perverse trout behavior strangely comforting.)

Since the day that Bob Lamm introduced me to the versatility of the beetle, I have not felt unprepared on any trout stream. Regardless of the species or size of the bugs trout may be eating, I no longer am daunted by the inadequacy of my collection of dry flies. I simply tie on a beetle.

Sometimes I almost feel guilty. Sometimes beetles work so well it seems like cheating.

Other times? Well, pattern anxiety, I've decided, is incurable anyway.

MIDGE PHOBIA

This trout was feeding with metronome regularity in the quick water at the head of the pool, the no-nonsense sipping rise of a decent-sized fish. The narrow run offered a long drag-free float on a riffled surface. Plenty of room for a backcast. I tied on a #14 Light Cahill, the precise imitation of the mayflies that were hatching sparsely on my little New England stream that day.

Duck soup, I thought.

The trout ignored a dozen perfect floats. Twice he rose within a foot of my fly.

I changed to a small beetle imitation, my ace in the hole. No dice. Ditto a Wulff, Adams, and, in desperation, a Variant. I tried an ant and a rusty spinner. Uh uh.

Perhaps he was feeding on emerging nymphs. I greased my leader and replaced the dry fly with an unweighted Hare's Ear, the closest thing I had. When the trout—which I had by now decided was a brown of fifteen or sixteen inches—spurned the emerger, fished both dead-drift and with a twitch, I replaced it with a weighted nymph. Same story.

I reeled in and sat to watch. The fish continued to feed. I followed the course of a natural mayfly tumbling through his lane. He rose beside it. The natural, like my various imitations, drifted on through.

Then I knew. It had happened too many times before. I waded into the water and bent over until my face was only a few inches from the surface. It was peppered with insects. They were black and small and abundant—less than a quarter-inch long, with a single pair of wings.

Diptera.

Midges.

Increasingly over the years I have encountered the same problem on my favorite eastern trout streams—trout gorging on microscopic insects and ignoring everything else.

I responded to this angling conundrum that day the same way I always did. I cast toward that midge-selective trout the only thing I had left that could bring me a measure of satisfaction— a sharply barbed expletive. Then I abandoned him and went searching for a fish that was willing to play fair.

I knew about midges. I had seen my rivers and ponds pocked with the tiny dimples of rising trout that ignored all conventional insect imitations. I had talked with fishermen who claimed to use midge flies with fabulous success, although I secretly suspected them of engaging me in some kind of purist one-upmanship.

Midge fishing was too much of a hassle. Midges were just too small—too small for my banana fingers to tie, too small to knot onto a leader tippet, too small to see floating on the surface. The tippets themselves were too frail for my typical heavy-handedness. Even accepting the possibility of their importance in a trout's diet and the skill of the fisherman who successfully imitated them, midge fishing simply wasn't worth it for me.

This all changed one chilly March afternoon. I had spent the morning bumping nymphs along the bottom of the Y Pool of the Swift River, one of our few twelve-month Massachusetts trout rivers. I had lots of company. Catch-and-release-minded fly fishermen from all over the Commonwealth flock to the Swift and congregate at the Y Pool, where incredibly selective rainbows up to twenty inches long live and feed year-round. There were about a dozen of us there that day, too many, really, for the limited space. But it was the only game in town.

A little after noontime the trout began to surface-feed, dotting the water with dimpling little riseforms. No insect was visible on the surface. A dozen fishermen stripped in and began to poke around their fly boxes. With a sinking feeling of deja vu I tied on the smallest thing I had, a #20 Blue-Winged Olive. When I cast it over one of the feeders, it looked like a porcupine carcass floating down the river. The trout, of course, ignored it.

Within a few minutes, the fly caster standing next to me was into a trout. The rest of us frowned and pretended not to notice him. Soon he caught another. Then another. And for the next two hours of the afternoon rise, that one fisherman must have released eight or ten fat rainbows, while the rest of us caught absolutely nothing.

Finally I couldn't stand it. "Hey, friend," I said. "Do you know magic or something?"

"Not magic," he said. "Midges."

"How small?"

"Twenty-eight."

I muttered something that was intended to be unintelligible, but he roll-cast his fly to me. "See for yourself," he said.

It appeared to be little more than a black thread body with a couple sparse turns of black hackle. A #28 hook offers little space for art.

I went home skunked. But my competitive juices were flowing.

The first challenge was tying the little devils. I chose ring-eye dry-fly hooks, which provide a wider bite than hooks with turned-down eyes, and allow the use of the easier clinch knot for fastening to the leader tippet. I selected 6/0 black thread, the finest I had. Finding no suitable hackles in my fly-tying kit, I settled on black deer hair as the material of choice. I clipped off about a dozen fibers, matched up the tips, and tied in a short tail. Then I wound the thread forward under the extended deer hair to a point just behind the eye of the hook. There I snugged down the deer hair over the shank, leaving a hump of hair between bend and eye as a body. At the eye of the hook the hair flared. I clipped this short and also clipped out all but three or four tail hairs. It made a buggy little morsel with all the good floating properties of hollow deer hair.

It took me less than ten minutes to tie it. I made several more, using a variety of colors (natural, white, and black deer hair with matching thread color) and hook sizes (20 to 28) and experimenting with the size and shape of the clipped flared hair at the head of the fly. I even managed to fashion spinner imitations with spent wings.

I arrived at the Y Pool two days later, armed and eager. I added a length of 7X tippet to my leader with a silent prayer of thanks to the man who invented the surgeon's knot. Then I fumbled in my box of fresh-tied midges. I lost two of them in the river before I remembered my hemostat. Nipping the tiny fly between the jaws of that most useful medical instrument and peering through my cheaters, I made short order of knotting the fly to the tippet with a clinch knot.

I cast it toward a riser. Beyond its butt, the sixteen feet of leader and fly melted from sight on the barely riffled surface. The trout rose about six feet downstream of where I guessed my fly was floating. I didn't strike. Belatedly, it occurred to me that perhaps the rise had come to my invisible midge. I lifted my rod and when the fly moved I realized that I had raised the fish.

Seeing the fly, I realized, would be impossible. But if I knew approximately where it was, I could strike at a rise. So I broke off a tiny piece of the white stick-on Orvis strike indicator that I use when nymphing and attached it to my leader three feet up from the fly. When I made my next cast, I still couldn't see the fly. But the strike indicator showed me approximately where it floated, and when the fish rose I lifted my rod tip sharply and quickly. Too quickly. The hook failed to set. With the tiny midge hook, a trout must be allowed time to close his jaws on it before the hook can be set.

I remembered what Bighorn guide Bill Rohrbacher once told me: When a good-sized trout rises to a small dry fly, say "big brown trout" to yourself before setting the hook.

Already, however, I felt I had succeeded. My midge imitation had raised two trout in two casts.

Three tries later, I rose another. I muttered "big brown trout" and then, with all the delicacy of a rail splitter, I set the hook. It implanted itself firmly somewhere in the trout's mouth. But the wispy 7X tippet snapped.

After several more missed strikes and one more bust-off, I managed to steady my nerves enough to raise my rod tip deliberately and gently against the strike. The crimson-cheeked rainbow that came to my net five minutes later, my tiny deerhair midge a mere speck in his lip, hooked me permanently on midge fishing.

I landed several more that afternoon, bragging rainbows that ranged from fourteen to seventeen inches, even with my typically low strike-to-catch ratio.

The others sharing the Y Pool with me were all skunked, and when the fisherman next to me asked, "Whatcha using?" I replied, perhaps too smugly, "Midges."

Entomologically, "midges" refer to Diptera, the order of two-winged flies comprised of such critters as mosquitoes and gnats.

To fishermen, a midge is anything on a #22 or smaller hook—that is, anything too small to see on the water or handle comfortably. Ants and several species of mayfly fall into this category.

Researchers have taken stomach samples from trout in eastern streams and ponds, where acid rain and pollutants have, in many cases, virtually eradicated mayflies. The scientists conclude that Diptera and, in season, other minutiae such as ants, have become predominant trout food. This makes sense. Diptera hatch year-round, and they seem to thrive in waters that are virtually sterile of other aquatic insect life.

Imitating Diptera, in my experience, is primarily a matter of size first, color second, and, a distant third, shape. Almost anything tiny and black will catch trout that are keyed on black midges, for example.

I have experimented with my little deerhair midge. I have found that clipping the flare of hair at the eye of the hook down to a little round nub usually works best. On occasion clipping off the entire tail, so the fly tends to ride vertically in the water like a pupa, will bring more strikes. Sometimes twitching them beneath the surface, nymphlike, does the trick. I continue to tie them with tails and flared heads and then perform customized streamside alterations as conditions seem to warrant.

Delicacy is the byword in midge fishing—delicate casting, delicate hook-setting, delicate equipment. I use a nine-foot graphite rod for a 4-weight line and long (up to sixteen-foot) leaders with two- or three-foot 7X tippets (shorter tippets, lacking stretch, snap more readily than longer ones). I still break off fish with heavy-handed regularity, but once I succeed in hooking them I have found that this outfit has enough guts to bring twenty-inch trout to the net before they are dangerously exhausted.

Since conquering midge phobia on the Swift River, I have found more and more opportunities to fish midges in their various forms in rivers and ponds East and West. Flashy #22 midge nymphs bumped along the bottom of the Frying Pan turned out to be the fly of choice for the gluttonous rainbows that live there. On ponds, the same imitation, cast out, allowed to sink, then twitched toward the surface sometimes is the only thing that will work. At other times, both on still and moving water, the "smutting" little riseforms of nymphing trout indicate they are feeding on midge pupae suspended vertically in the surface film. Tiny hackled flies without tails can fool these fish.

Some status-minded anglers seem to regard midge fishing as another refinement of the fine art of fly fishing for trout, one more rung on the evolutionary ladder up from lowly worm dunkers and hardware heavers. I see it in more pragmatic terms, and I have confirmed my view on many trout waters from Walden Pond to the Bighorn River where fishermen curse the picky appetites and exaggerated selectivity of rising trout: Midges will often catch trout when nothing else will.

Given the choice, I've decided I'd rather catch em'.

THE HAIR OF THE DEER
Part I
Tap's Trout Bugs

I pegged him right away. An Expert. He sported a black beret studded with tiny cream and ginger nymphs and a couple of artful Atlantic salmon flies, a neatly trimmed white mustache, and a bulging Orvis vest.

And he was good. He cast with economical grace, and during the twenty minutes that I watched him work the shady pool downstream from the power line, he took three foot-long-plus trout—rainbows, I guessed. This was at midday on an August Saturday on the most heavily fished mile of trout river in New England—or maybe the world: the fly-fishing-only catch-and-release section of the Swift River in central Massachusetts. There, the water flows from the bottom of the Windsor Dam at the foot of the Quabbin Reservoir as clear and as cold as a well-shaken martini, and it harbors one of the heaviest—and most sophisticated—populations of trout anywhere.

But this Expert was having no apparent trouble catching them. After he released his third trout, I called to him. "Hey! What're you using?"

He looked up and saw me for the first time. He smiled, reeled in, and sloshed over to where I sat on the bank.

He flopped down beside me and produced a straight-stemmed pipe and a pouch of tobacco from somewhere in the depths of his fishing vest. He loaded it up, and as he set fire to it, he mumbled, "Small Pheasant Tail." He peered at me, took my measure, and explained, "Nymphs."

"How small?"

"Quite small. Twenty."

He offered me several other observations, many of them in Latin, before he knocked out his pipe and wandered off upstream.

Halfheartedly, I busted off the #16 Adams I'd been using and tied on the tiniest nymph I had with me. It looked like a Great Blue Heron compared to the Pheasant Tail the Expert had showed me, and the trout treated it as if it were a member of that species.

"Didn't want to fish nymphs anyway," I mumbled—out loud, I think.

The smallest, sparsest dry fly in my vest that day was a #18 Blue-Winged Olive. I tied it on and waded, without much optimism, into the glide downstream from the Y Pool. I spotted a few sporadic dimples within casting range. In half an hour I managed to induce two splashy refusals.

"Midges, then," I thought, with a sinking feeling.

I fumbled in the pockets of my vest. I found a box of tarpon flies. No midges. Oh, well.

"If I'm not going to catch any fish," I thought next, "I might as well not catch them on something I can see."

I consulted my fly boxes. I carry hundreds of flies with me. None of them ever seems to be the one I need. My eye stopped at a concoction of natural-colored deer hair on a #12 hook. My father had given me half a dozen of these crude, vaguely buggy-looking creatures a couple years earlier. He called them "trout bugs," and he swore they were deadly on the brook trout native

83

to his New Hampshire streams. "Fish it like a bass bug," he said. "Drives 'em absolutely nuts."

I remember searching his face for that familiar twinkle in his eye that would tell me he was joking. I didn't see it. The man was serious.

I exercised a full measure of filial respect by not telling Dad who I thought was absolutely nuts, dutifully tucked his "trout bugs" in with my real flies, and then unfilially proceeded to ignore them.

"Why not?" I thought. If nothing else, I would show my utter disdain for those snooty Swift River trout.

I tied on a trout bug and cast it cross-stream, swinging it around on a tight line in a wide arc so that it cut a wake across the smooth surface of the water.

"Skittered trout bugs," Dad had told me, "work for trout the same way a fly tied with a Portland Creek hitch works for salmon. Maybe even better."

On the Swift River that August Saturday, the trout bug looked like a muskrat swimming across the current. So I wasn't ready for the splashy strike that came on my second cast, and I snatched it away from the smallish trout that catapulted clean out of the water in its frustration. I missed the next strike, too, but hooked the third, a chunky eleven-inch brookie.

My skittered trout bug continued to draw attention, and in the next hour, even though I missed connections on two-thirds of the strikes the bug induced, I managed to land and release two more brookies, a small brown, and a fourteen-inch rainbow. And when I spotted a steady riser upstream of me, I cast the bug above him and let it drift down to him on a dragless float. He pounced on it.

I want to make no extravagant claim for the trout bug. Most of the time on most rivers trout bugs, like everything else in my arsenal, don't work.

84

But they are fun to use, and sometimes I'm in the mood for skittering and twitching them across the currents of logjammed streams. Sometimes, even, trout dart and slash at them as if they were legitimate trout flies.

On the Pine River, Dad's favorite trout stream, the brookies go for his bugs in preference to every other fly we've tried. And I've tried them all, in a futile effort to prove that dumb trout, not magic flies, explain it. Maybe those Pine River brookies spurn cleverly tied mayfly and terrestrial imitations because they're stupid, I don't know. But they do prefer those trout bugs. Hatch-matching be damned, is the message. Drag one of those deer-hair critters nearby.

One of the things I like best about trout bugs is that they're easy to tie. Even with his arthritic fingers, my father can knock off a dozen perfect bugs in an hour. He wraps the shank of a #12 dry-fly hook with a peacock herl. Then he lays a pinch of deer hair, clipped to the proper length, over the top and ties it down fore and aft. He snips off the excess hair at the eye of the hook, leaving a small bristly head and a short tail of the fine hairs at the butt. He ties 'em in yellow, red, black, white, natural, bicolored, whatever. Trout seem not to notice the color.

Trout bugs, by the way, are absolute killer bluegill flies. I leave a few bristles sticking out at the head for bluegills. They look like legs, I suppose. They give the bug some additional action when twitched on the surface beside a patch of lily pads. Crappies and the occasional bass gobble them, too.

I still have trouble taking them seriously for trout, though, which probably says more about me than it does about trout.

My success with the funny-looking trout bugs seems to offend the fly-fishing sensibilities of most anglers I run into, which is another one of the reasons I still occasionally use them. Give me an audience and I'll tie on a trout bug. If it fails to raise a fish, I can always dismiss it as an experiment. And when it works, my observers, I like to think, are forced to conclude, "That guy must be a helluva fisherman, to handicap himself with a fly like that and still catch trout."

Then, naturally, they've got to examine the silly thing. I always expect them to laugh. Strangely, they don't. Instead, they hold it up to the light, pursing their lips and clucking. Then they nod. "Caddis," they might opine. Or, "Looks like a hopper," or, "emerging nymph, that's the ticket."

I don't know why trout eat them. Maybe they really do look edible. I have caught trout with Old Gold filters in their stomachs. Or maybe they look so alien to trout waters, and, when skittered, they behave so strangely that the fish are provoked into striking out of anger or aggression. Other species such as bass and pickerel certainly behave that way, why not trout?

It doesn't really matter. I'll be damned if I'm going to tell those people who watch me use them my reasons.

I'm not going to tell them that it's a joke.

THE HAIR OF THE DEER
Part II
Tap's Bass Bugs

When I was a kid, largemouth bass were the most glamorous fish in my constricted fishing neighborhood. I liked largemouths better than hatchery trout, eels, pickerel, and calico bass, the other exotic species available. I fished for bass with minnows, nightcrawlers, and crawfish, Johnson Spoons, Hula Poppers, and Jitterbugs.

Largemouths, sometimes, were big. That's what I liked. That plus the fact that they were a "game fish."

My angling tastes have evolved—or regressed, I'm not sure which—since my childhood. But next to dry-fly trout, I still love bass the best. The only difference is that now I'll catch my bass on topwater deer-hair bugs, cast with a fly rod, or I won't bother trying to catch them at all.

When my father invented his deer-hair bass bug, he salvaged bass fishing for me.

Deer hair is about the most useful and versatile fly-tying material, natural or synthetic, known to man. Each hair is hollow, a virtually unsinkable flotation device. When a pinch of deer hair is snugged down tight onto the shank of a hook, it flares out and spins around and can be snipped and sculpted into any imaginable shape. That's its magic. I've used deer hair to create workable midges on #24 hooks for trout. I've also used it on tarpon flies. And just about everything in between, from crab flies for permit to Muddler Minnows and beetles and ants.

Trimmed deer hair, I believe, feels more lifelike in a fish's mouth than cork, wood, plastic, or metal. Properly designed deer-hair flies are lighter and more easily cast with a fly rod than comparably sized ones made of harder materials.

Best of all, maybe, any fisherman with connections in the deer-hunting fraternity can obtain a lifetime supply of deer hair free for the asking. Bucktails might cost the fly tier something, but not a hunk of hide.

My father has been fooling around with deer hair since Joe Messinger created his famous Meadow Frog, and I was brought up to believe that fly-rod bugging was the most exciting—and, under the right conditions, the most effective—way to fish for black bass, largemouth or small. Those Messinger Frogs caught bass, all right. But their bulky shape made them about as easy to cast as a soggy boot. Dad experimented with a more stream-lined version of the hair frog by leaving off the legs and pronounced it an improvement.

Tap, as everyone knows, is an inveterate tinkerer. So he continued his quest for the perfect bass bug. He tried cork and balsa and molded plastic, and found them all wanting. For a while he settled on the Roy Yates Deacon, an all-white floating first cousin to the Muddler. But the Deacon failed to kick up enough fuss on the water to satisfy my father. "The ideal bass bug," he proclaimed, "would be as durable as wood, cast at least as easily as a streamer fly, and float forever. Most of all, it should cause a real ruckus when you twitch it. Ergo, the ideal bass bug must be made of deer hair."

The product of Dad's trials and errors is a bass bug that is both simple and devastatingly effective. Its most significant feature is its flat face, which makes a satisfying *Glug!* when it's twitched. "It's got to burble, not pop," asserts my father, who can expostulate for hours on the subject, "and for the proper burble you need a flat face, neither concave nor convex. And deer hair. Hard materials simply don't give you the right burble. For one thing, they ride too high on the surface. See, deer-hair bugs will soak up a little water, so that they sit lower than the hard-bodied ones. This is the key to achieving the perfect glug. It will attract them, not startle them."

Dad's bass bug tapers gracefully back from its flat face to a bushy hair tail. No legs, no wings. With its streamlined, aerodynamic shape, I can cast it comfortably all day with a medium-weight fly rod. When it gets too waterlogged, I just squeeze it dry.

And, oh, that glug!

Dad ties his bugs in a variety of highly visible color combinations, mainly to satisfy his own artistic needs. "I doubt if the bass give a hoot about color," he says, "so I just make 'em pretty. It's not as if they're supposed to imitate mice or frogs or wounded minnows. It's the movement and the glug that gets 'em, that's what counts."

Pickerel eat them, too, and northern pike and bluefish eat larger versions. "Any color is good for pickerel," says Dad, "as long as it's yellow."

There are two distinct steps in tying one of Tap's deer-hair bass bugs. First, he packs the flared deer hair onto the hook as densely as possible. He begins with the tail, which is made from deer hair a little softer than the usual run, fine at the tips but hollow enough to flare out at the butt end and create a smooth connection between tail and body. To create the body of the bug, he takes a pinch of hair about the thickness of a drinking straw between his thumb and forefinger, lays it diagonally across the top of the hook shank beginning at the tail butts, and snugs it down tightly with a couple of turns of 00 nylon. The hair flares and spins around the hook. He keeps repeating this process, shoving each segment of spun hair back hard against the previous one, working his way forward until the hook is full and looks like a hairy ball.

Then he removes the hook from the vise and begins the second step, which he likens to hedge trimming. Using extra-sharp straight-bladed scissors, he clips the bottom flat and as close to the shank of the hook as possible. He tapers the top and sides back evenly to a point at the tail.

He can make three in an hour. One will last forever, unless too many pickerel glom onto it.

Bass bugs are most effective when fished on calm, shady water near structures in relatively shallow areas. I cast as close to weed beds, sunken logs, overhanging brush, or rocks as I can, let the bug sit quietly for a moment, then give it a sharp yank. The *glug!* it makes will get the attention of whatever bass is lurking nearby. I let it sit, burble it again, and so forth. The timing of this glug-rest-glug sequence depends on the species. Largemouths seem to prefer a more leisurely pace, so I use longer rest periods between glugs for them than I do for smallmouths. Pickerel favor a fast, steady glug-glug-glug retrieve. Their torpedo-like charge and crashing strike are more than worth the frayed leaders and tattered bugs caused by their needle-sharp teeth.

Blaine Moores and I fished the Belgrade Lakes last June with Dave Barnes. The smallmouths were on the beds. Prime bassing time for catch-and-release-minded fishermen.

Dave is a licensed Maine bass guide and a veteran of tournaments all over the country. He wins more than his share of them. I figured I'd learn a few things.

He swooped up to the dock in his shiny bass boat. It bristled with spinning rods. Blaine and I were waiting for him. Each of us had an 8-weight fly rod in one hand and a plastic box of deer-hair bugs in the other.

Dave took one look and rolled his eyes. "What in hell is that?" he said.

"Fly rod." We climbed into the boat.

He shrugged. "Well, I've got plenty of gear. You can use my stuff."

He took us a couple hundred yards down the lake. We stopped over a shoal. Under five feet of water I could see a scattering of boulders on the gravel bottom. Prime spawning grounds.

Dave picked up one of his spinning rods and showed me the lure he had snapped onto the swivel: a lead jig with a chartreuse rubber skirt. I forget what he called it. "I've been killing 'em on this thing," he said. "See, you cast it out and drag it onto a bed. The bass picks it up in his mouth. Then you rip his lips."

He held the rod to me. I shook my head. "I'll try this," I said.

A two-pound smallmouth ate my deer-hair bug on my first cast.

Before our two days together ended, Dave Barnes and I had debated the relative merits of bass and trout, fly rod and spinning, until we began to repeat ourselves. I doubt if I convinced him of anything. I know he didn't change my mind.

Because this is what I believe: Under the right circumstances, a man with a fly rod can catch as many bass—and as many large ones—with a deer-hair bug as can a spin fisherman with a rubber worm, jig and pig, spinner bait, stick bait, or anything else.

The operative words are "right circumstances." I want calm, shady water. Dawn or dusk or one of those soft misty summer days. I want shallow water with lots of what the tournament boys call "structure." Brush that hangs over the shoreline, submerged trees, weed beds. For smallmouths, lots of rocks.

If the bass are near the surface, I'll catch them on bugs. Guaranteed.

Not that the other guys won't. But I'll have more fun doing it. Also guaranteed.

Dusk. Bullfrogs grumble from the shore. Swallows swoop and dive. Soft evening mists hover over the little pond. Bluegills spat in the shallows. Two men drift in a canoe. Water drips from the blade of the paddle. The shoreline darkens as the sun settles behind the trees.

The man with the paddle points toward shore, whispers something. The man with the fly rod nods, false-casts once, twice. A narrow loop of line rolls toward the fallen tree that lies leafless in the water. Silence. Then a glug, as audible to the men as the bullfrog's burp. A moment of silence, another glug.

A sudden implosion in the water. The man with the rod strikes back. The man with the paddle grins and mutters, "There! I knew it!"

The largemouth leaps, crashes to the water, leaps again. He bulldogs, striving for the tangle of underwater branches where he had been lurking. He's no match for the fly rod. Five minutes later the man with the rod seizes the fish's lower jaw between thumb and crooked forefinger, hoists him high. "Four pounds," he says.

"Closer to five," says his companion.

He disengages the hook, returns the fish to the water. The two men gingerly turn in their seats. They swap implements.

They will do this well into the night and regret their time was so short.

Part 4
THE FISH-TIL-YOU-PUKE SYNDROME

Dear Dad: Andy and I drove down to the Farmington yesterday. Arrived about ten ayem. Stream full of rising trout. Equally full of wading fly casters. Hard to say who outnumbered whom. We wedged ourselves in among them. Fish feeding all day. Started with number eighteen Blue-Winged Olives, worked through all my fly boxes, wet, damp, and dry, finished up eleven hours later with midges, twenty-fours, still wondering what they were eating. Stayed in the river literally nonstop until dark. Caught seven small browns, the only dumb ones I could find. Love, Bill.

Dear Son: Nobody has a bladder with an eleven-hour capacity, nor does anyone your age have a back that can bear up *literally* nonstop that long. I'm disappointed in you. "Literally" means just that. You meant "figuratively," or perhaps, "virtually." Call yourself a writer? Love, Dad.

Dad: I used the word "literally" correctly. Bill.

Bill: Then there's something else wrong with you. Dad.

On our annual midsummer western trout-bombing mission,
Andy and I rise at dawn every day. We don't want to miss the
morning spinner fall. We fish beetles for bank-sippers hard
through midday, which takes us into the evening hatch of
sulphurs or midges or caddis. We never eat lunch, unless we're
with guides who insist on it. It's generally around midnight
when we drag ourselves into the only all-night diner in town.
We eat good Montana steer beef, return to our digs to tie flies,
and we're up at dawn the next day.

We follow this schedule every day for the entire two weeks.
We find it exhilarating. We never feel tired, hungry, or thirsty.
It's simply what we do when we fish for trout.

Nobody believes we do this. Not *literally*. But we do.

Andy and I are sober, sensible, responsible middle-aged men.
At least we think so. We are not unaware of how our behavior
looks to others. It looks compulsive, suicidal, obsessive to the
point of psychosis. It looks pretty much the same to us. We've
tried to analyze it. We've come up with two conclusions.

First, our partnership wouldn't survive unless we shared this
trout-intensity equally, to the same extreme degree.

Second, we *do* know about leisurely fishing. We just don't
associate it with trout.

Fly fishing for trout, we acknowledge, is our obsession. We
will fly, drive, hike, and wade incredible distances to find trout
to cast a fly to. We endure blazing heat, or sleet or rain or wind
or snow, without complaint—and it doesn't matter much
whether the fishing's good or bad. In fact, the worse it is the
more obsessive we tend to become.

Fishing for other species, on the other hand, is our
recreation. We take it slow and easy. We like to paddle a canoe
or a float tube around the rim of a bass pond and cast bugs

toward shore. We make a couple of Cape Cod bluefish-on-a-fly-rod runs each summer. We wade the Indianhead for shad in May. Sometimes we bring a sack of bluegills home from Bare Hill Pond. We filet them together while sharing a bottle of decent Chardonnay, and Andy deep fries them and we gorge on them the same night with another Chardonnay.

On a bass pond, we stop fishing to admire the angling technique of a heron. We try to identify the warblers in the bushes and the ducks in the coves. We pause to watch the setting sun paint the sky, and sometimes Andy toots his harmonica in counterpoint to the grumps of bullfrogs and the trills of night birds, and we pronounce ourselves healthy after all.

An excursion for a species other than trout is maybe the only evidence we can submit that we have not—*literally*—gone round the bend.

NEW ENGLAND
VARIATIONS ON THEMES
BY VIVALDI

1. Spring *May is the Cruelest Month*

I know a housewife who once won a shopping spree at the local
Stop & Shop. At the appointed hour, with the assistant man-
ager holding a stopwatch and a storeful of patrons to cheer her
on, she was given a shopping cart and five minutes to fill it with
anything she wanted from the shelves. She got to keep everything in the cart.

"It was awful," she told me afterward. "I careened up and
down the aisles, barely looking at all the stuff on the shelves. I
couldn't decide what to take. When I grabbed at something I
knocked it onto the floor and couldn't make up my mind
whether to scoop it up or keep going. I wasted almost a minute
just trying to decide between the rib roasts and the T-bone
steaks. I spent way too much time in the canned goods section,
and I never did make it to the gourmet aisle. I ended up with
lots of cheap, bulky things like whole-wheat bread and potato
chips and paper towels. When it was over, and I realized all I
had missed, I sat right down on the floor and cried."

I nodded sympathetically. I knew exactly how she felt. It's a devilish form of Oriental torture, to have so much placed within your grasp but to lack the time and resources to take it all.

The very abundance of it is paralyzing.

I win a shopping spree every spring. My New England lakes, ponds, rivers, and streams are my supermarket. My time limit is thirty-one days, the month of May. I squander too much of it agonizing over the abundance of my options, fumbling my chances, and, as the days sift away, mourning lost opportunities.

It's now the middle of April. The streams are still too high and cold for good fly fishing, but they're coming down fast. Truckloads of flaccid trout have been dumped into the ponds, and busloads of fishermen ring the shorelines.

Andy and I drove to Scargo Pond down on the Cape last Sunday. The usual flotilla of watercraft littered its surface, and it was ringed with spin casters and worm dunkers, but trout were making pockmarks all over its glassy skin when we got there. It's what we had hoped for. We could catch a boatload with midge nymphs twitched beneath the surface. It would be a good way to shake out our angling kinks.

We lugged Andy's canoe to the beach and began to assemble our gear. We fumbled around a lot. It was our first expedition of the year. We were pretty excited. Every trout in the pond was showing himself.

We bent to our task, stringing rods, remaking last year's leaders, selecting flies, renewing our acquaintance with knots, and when we were done we looked up. While our attention had been diverted, a northeast breeze had begun to chop whitecaps into the water and blow hard little raindrops at us from a suddenly leaden sky.

We bit off our flies, put away our rods, hoisted the canoe back onto the car, and drove home.

But May is around the corner. I feel that familiar paralysis gripping me again. Everything looks delicious. How can I, just this once, have it all? I don't want to make the hard choices. I want a bottomless shopping cart, a broken stopwatch. I want to prowl all the aisles of my outdoor supermarket and fill my wagon with all the fishy delicacies on the New England shelves.

Alas, where to start? Sebago or Moosehead, Winnipesaukee or Quabbin, for landlocked salmon, and quick, before the surface water warms up and *Salmo sebago* heads for the depths where wire-draggers are the only ones who can get to him. I'll cast streamers—Grey Ghosts and Supervisors and Warden's Worries and Edson Dark Tigers—toward the boulders along the windward shore and troll a tandem combination behind me. Short line in high chop, a long line on calm water. Maybe I'll pick up a laker or a squaretail as a bonus. If so, it'll be a big one.

Salmon don't come easy. I've spent entire weekends without getting a strike. To do it right, I'll have to invest several days.

And there's the dilemma. Because time spent on salmon is time lost from the best trout fishing of the New England year. And I love trout fishing the most. In May real mayflies still hatch on the Deerfield and the Farmington and the Housie, and a float-tuber can usually count on an evening rise in any one of three hundred Cape ponds.

Yes, but . . .

But in May the warmwater fish move into the shallows— saucer-sized bluegills and crappies as big as dinner plates and pickerel as long as my daughter's leg. In May the shad invade the Indianhead and the Merrimack. In May the largemouths of Bare Hill Pond and the Charles River take up their posts under

100

waterlogged trees. In May the smallmouths of Winnipesaukee and the Belgrades scratch out spawning beds along the shores. In May big landlocked salmon come to dry flies and nymphs on the Magalloway and the West Branch of the Penobscot and Grand Lake Stream. Just like trout, only bigger and grander.

I want it all.

It's a beautiful wicked month, May in New England. Thirty-one days simply isn't enough for any normally greedy fisherman. The best you get is a bite, not a meal. Most of the goodies get left on the shelves or spilled on the floor. The poet had it wrong. May, not April, is the cruelest month.

2. Summer *Dog Days*

When we had to wait in line for half an hour at the boat landing to launch our canoe, we should have known.

Andy and I had lashed my Grumman atop my wagon just as the sky was beginning to pinken in the east. Fortified with a Thermos of coffee, we put the sun at our backs and slipped onto the Mass Pike. Destination: a big lake nestled in the foothills of the Berkshires, where Andy once won a bass tournament, and where, we had heard, northern pike and tiger muskies had taken hold. We had lemonade and iced tea in the cooler. I smuggled my transistor radio along, since the Sox were still in the pennant race and were playing the Indians in the afternoon. I didn't think Andy would approve, but I was betting that if the Sox were hitting better than the bass he'd allow it.

Better than mowing the lawn, better even than swinging in a hammock, on a lazy July Saturday.

Ah, we should have known.

We sat in line and waited, sipping the lukewarm dregs of our coffee while the sun climbed into the summer sky. The vehicle in front of us was a flashy new convertible containing half a dozen teenagers in skimpy swimwear. It was hauling a trailer carrying a sleek torpedo-shaped speedboat. A motor the size of an old-fashioned washing machine was mounted on the transom.

Finally we paid our fee, off-loaded the canoe, and I drove off to find a parking space in the crowded lot while Andy strung his rod. When I got back and shoved off, I said to Andy, "Which way?"

It was, I knew, a good question. A sand beach curved off to the left of the boat launch. It was already liberally dotted with sun bathers and swimmers, and from its direction emanated a constant low-level din, a mix of the shrieks and laughs of children, the screams of their parents, the throb of rock music, and the shrill of lifeguards' whistles. Out on the lake sailboats skittered around like a hatch of water bugs. Powerboats carved noisy white scrolls into the blue surface of our fishing lake. The shoreline was rimmed with cottages, each with a dock perched on stilts over the water, and at each dock more watercraft were moored and more nearly naked people swam and lounged.

It was, all in all, a typical big New England lake on a steamy July Saturday.

We certainly should have known.

I paddled past a long row of cottages. Around a point we came upon another bathing beach, this one the waterfront of a girl's summer camp. Beyond that we found a shallow, lily-padded cove.

"Here," said Andy. "This is a good spot. I did good here."

Andy began to cast a bass bug toward shore. It took only a couple minutes for the water-skiers to find us. Their game was to see how close the kid on skis could come to the older guys in the funny little canoe without actually colliding with it. He was able to come very close. I managed to keep the bow pointed into the wake and we did not swamp.

When those kids tired of their game, the sailboats found us. There were three of them, and perched up on the forward bulkhead of each one was a lithe girl in a bikini who waved gleefully to us as they slid past.

It was distracting.

Andy and I rolled on the wakes, waved back at the girls, and didn't say much. It was hard to hear each other over the noise that boomed over the water at us. We lasted an hour. Then I paddled back, and we lifted the canoe onto the wagon and drove home.

We caught the last couple innings in Andy's back yard.

The dog days. We should have known.

"Fairhaven Bay," I said to Andy after the Sox blew it in the ninth. "We should've gone there. It's where my father used to take me on July Saturdays when I was a kid . . ."

Fairhaven Bay bulges like an aneuryism on the gently meandering artery of the Sudbury River. It was never a wilderness experience, fishing the bay. Recreational canoeists and the occasional powerboat zigzagged around it, even thirty years ago. It's a little more crowded now. But, hell, Fairhaven Bay sits smack in the population center of Massachusetts, an hour's drive west of Boston or east of Worcester.

Even so, it's kind of pretty there. Meadow and marsh border the bay, a broad floodplain that keeps civilization distant from its banks. On most days, unless the wind is wrong, you can't hear the whine of the traffic on Route 2. There's a small island where Dad and I used to dig up Indian arrowheads after our picnic lunch. Herons and ducks and geese and a rich assortment of shorebirds flock there as if they knew it was a bird sanctuary.

I was probably ten the day Dad and I caught a dozen different species of fish in Fairhaven Bay without lifting the anchor.

We didn't set out to see how many kinds of fish we could boat that day. We were after largemouth bass. We anchored in a weedy cove near the point where the bay narrows to resume its shape as a river. Dad was casting a small deer-hair bug toward the brush-clogged shoreline. I heaved a spinner-and-worm rig off the other side of the canoe toward the deep water.

I hit a school of white perch immediately. Then, on successive casts, I landed a crappie and a yellow perch. Meanwhile, two hand-sized bluegills and then a small sunfish tried to eat Dad's bug. So before we had settled our fannies in the canoe we had caught five different species of fish.

Panfish, nothing special. Dad and I were after bass, and when he hooked still another chunky bluegill he replaced the bug he was using with a larger one. "There are bass under those bushes," he said, "but I can't keep the bluegills away."

By this time I had landed a few more perch and crappies. Then I caught a pond shiner. "Do you realize," I said, showing Dad the shiner, "that we've been here maybe fifteen minutes and this makes six different kinds of fish we've caught?"

He shrugged. "We haven't gotten what we came for," he said.

"How many do you think we can catch? Huh?"

He grinned. "Why don't you rig up with a gob of those worms you insisted on bringing and see what's feeding on the bottom? I want to catch a bass."

I began to catch horned pout. Finally Dad horsed in a smallish largemouth. A few casts later a pickerel charged out from under the bushes to attack his bug. I caught a sucker, another horned pout, then a small carp. Eleven species.

"Time to lift anchor," said Dad. "No big bass here. Let's stop wasting time and do some serious bassing."

"Wait," I said. "A few more minutes, please? I want to see if there's something else down there. Maybe we can make it an even dozen. Please?"

"Don't whine," he said.

He broke off his bug and tied on a plain hook, which he loaded up with worms. We both caught horned pout. I was about ready to concede when Dad's rod bowed so steeply and suddenly that the tip touched the water. "What the. . . ?" he muttered. Then he said, "Must be a bass." Then, "Big one, too."

His line sawed back and forth. "*Big* bass," he repeated through clenched teeth.

When he finally gained line and worked the fish close to the canoe, he began to laugh. "Skinniest bass I ever saw," he said, as he reached into the water with his knife to cut off an eel that must have been close to a yard long. "That's twelve," he said. "Your even dozen. Let's go catch some bass."

Andy swayed in his hammock, his eyes shut, an empty glass resting on his chest. "I wouldn't mind doing that," he said. "Jeez, a thirty-six inch eel?"

3. Fall *Raking Leaves*

Art picked at the burrs in Julie's ears. The little Springer rolled onto her back and pawed the air in protest. We sat with our backs against an old stone wall near the barway where Art's Jeep was parked and gazed toward the low-hanging November sun. Behind us the Ipswich swale rolled back toward the Atlantic marshes.

"Pretty good day," said Art.

"Two pheasants. Not bad."

"Shoulda had two others."

"If I'd been shooting decent, you mean," I said.

"*I* didn't say that." He scratched Julie's chin. "Same time next Saturday?"

"Goes without saying. Saturdays are for hunting."

"What about tomorrow?"

"Tomorrow? Tomorrow's Sunday, remember? What's to do? Rake up the oak leaves, maybe split some firewood. Worse comes to worse, I'll watch the Patriots get beat on the tube. No hunting on Sunday. It's the law."

"Trouble is," said Art, "for working stiffs like us, the same thing goes for Monday through Friday, too."

"All we've got is Saturday."

"Yup. Us and every other hunter in the state." He reached over and tapped my knee. "You want to go out tomorrow?"

"Love to. But we can't. Hunting's illegal."

"Fishing ain't."

Art came by at noon on that November Sunday. We hoisted my Grumman atop his Jeep and drove to—well, never mind. It's a pond near where I live in suburban Massachusetts. There are dozens just like it within an hour's drive from Boston. There, on a summer Sunday afternoon, a boatful of kids can fill a gunny sack with bluegills. When the sun sinks behind the trees, big largemouths move into the shallows to feed. Pickerel zing around in the weeds even under the high August sun.

It's fun, if you have a boatful of kids with you. It suits the spirit of the place in the summer. Everyone else on the pond has his Little League team with him, too.

On that Sunday in November, Art and I had the place to ourselves. It was a good start.

"I don't know about this," I told him. "November. Time for grouse and pheasants. Deer season around the corner. Take a look. The trees are bare. Even the water weeds are gone. It doesn't look right." I blew into my fists. "Doesn't feel right, either. The weather girl predicted snow tonight."

Art lost the coin toss, so he took the paddle. I stripped out some line and tossed a little rubber-legged bug in against the bushes that overhung the shoreline. I twitched it back slowly, just under the surface. Nothing.

I cast again and let the bug sink a little deeper. I knew it was a good spot. In the summer a three-pound bass lived under those bushes. Again, no strike.

"As I suspected," I said. "The fish are hibernating."

"Rather be raking leaves?"

"I'd rather be hunting," I said.

"Fish it deeper," suggested Art.

I pinched a tiny split shot onto the leader and cast again. With the sudden surge of the strike I momentarily forgot my numb fingers and the bulky sweater I was wearing under my windbreaker. For just an instant it could have been July. I brought a frisky bluegill to the boat. When I held him in my hand to unhook him, his body felt as cold as a frosted beer can.

I'd be lying if I said that the fishing that November day was as fast as it usually was on a soft June evening. And while the water didn't make ice in the guides, I did get chilled to my gizzard when a breeze sprang up in midafternoon. But between us Art and I caught about a dozen nice bluegills and three bass—none big—and two small pickerel.

It wasn't spectacular. By summer standards it was downright slow, and I was not tempted to sell my shotgun.

But my pond was a different place in November. No other fishermen, no swimmers, no water-skiers. No other boats whatsoever. The cottages along the shore were locked up, their windows boarded and their docks hauled up on shore.

The silence of the place is what we noticed. Just the dip of the paddle, now and then the splash of a fish. No mosquito hum, no bird song, no frog burp. No outboard motors, either, or transistor radios. It was so peaceful it was perfectly spooky.

Toward dusk a wedge of geese came honking overhead, low, wings set. Art raised his paddle and jammed the blade against his shoulder. He aimed it at the lead goose. "Bang," he said softly.

4. Winter *Voyeurism*

Thin yellow sunlight filters halfheartedly onto a new half-foot of snow. The red stuff in the thermometer stands about half an inch tall. The pine trees out back creak and crack in the sharp wind.

It is, in other words, a typical New England Saturday in January, and I'm happy to be indoors tying flies. When the phone rings, I let my machine take it.

"I know you're there," says Andy after my message tells him I'm not."

"Go away," I say to his voice.

"Answer the damn phone," he says. "I got a proposition."

I wheeze experimentally a couple times until I think I have it right. Then I pick up the telephone. "I got a cold," I croak.

"You do sound terrible," says Andy cheerfully. "You need some fresh air."

I cough for him. He chuckles. "Anyway, I got company," I say.

108

"Nice try. Get bundled up, pal. We're going ice fishing. Pick you up in half an hour."

"You know better," I say, desperate now. "I don't do ice fishing. Ice fishing is for masochists. I'm no masochist. Plenty of other things, granted, but not a masochist. So forget it."

But he has already hung up.

My attitude, which Andy has heard me try to defend many times, is this: There are any number of things that I would prefer to watch other people do than do myself. Running the Boston Marathon, sky diving, climbing into the ring with Mike Tyson. And ice fishing. I feel about ice fishing the same way I feel about hard work. I'm not afraid of it. I can watch other people do it for hours at a time.

Most sensible people, I believe, feel the same way. According to this compelling logic, Andy is not a sensible person. He keeps insisting that ice fishing is fun.

"Ice fishing," I amend, "is fun to watch."

"You're sick," diagnoses my partner the shrink. "You're a voyeur. You're a spectator, a sloth. You sit around on your fat duff smoking and drinking and eating onion-flavored potato chips. You, pal, typify the decline of America, the rotting away of the moral fiber of our great nation."

"Do you always have to make my behavior typify something?" I whine. "I just don't wanna go ice fishing."

"Ice fishing is great sport."

"It's a pretty good spectator sport," I say. "That's as far as I'll go. You get all the benefits, and none of the miseries, as a spectator."

My favorite place to watch others fish through the ice is Walden Pond, mainly because it's a five-minute drive from the warmth of my hearth. I wait until the sun has risen well into the sky and I have fortified myself with a leisurely breakfast and several cups of hot coffee. I gear myself minimally—cross-country skis or ice skates, depending on the surface of the pond. I lug with me no sack of tip-ups, no power auger, no bucket of bait, no skimmer, no cold lunch, no Thermos, no portable wind shelter.

By the time I get there, the pond is dotted with the masochists who have resolutely decided to spend the day squinting at tip-ups that will never tip up, and for whom a wind flag constitutes a successful outing.

Ice fishermen, I have found, in spite of their obvious maladjustments, are a sociable lot. They welcome company, and while they stand there leaning against the wind, stamping their feet and hugging their gloved hands under their armpits, they like to talk. At Walden they talk of the big brown trout that lure them there, eight- and ten-pounders that snap up dangled smelt once or twice every winter.

I've never met an ice fisherman who actually caught one of these fish. Most of them hardly ever catch anything. I'm the one who has all the luck when I go spectating. In my vicarious way, I hardly ever get skunked. Out on the pond, I flit from angler to angler, listening to his stories, checking out his equipment. I keep warm by moving around, and I'm always alert for a sudden dash by one of the figures on the ice. Propelled by skis or skates, I speed to the scene of the action. I get there in time to watch the ice angler shuck his gloves and finger his line as it runs through his hands. I doubt if he gets more excited than I do. My thrill, I'm convinced, equals his when he lands a fish.

And my fingers are dry and warm. His gloves usually land in a puddle of slush. He has to chop them out.

I spud and skim no holes. I impale no minnows on hooks, I tend no lines with frozen fingers. I'm mobile. I fish all over the pond. On a good day, I tend a hundred holes. When things are slow, I pack up no gear before skating back to my warm car to go looking for another pond where the flags might be flying. Sometimes I'll fish a dozen ponds in a single afternoon.

We lug Andy's ice-fishing gear through snowdrifts up to our crotches. We work up unhealthy sweats cutting holes through eleven inches of ice with his man-powered auger. We frost our fingers fumbling shiners out of his bait bucket and sticking hooks through their lips. We eat cold sandwiches and drink cold coffee. We haul in a couple of stiff twelve-inch pickerel.

Andy tells a few good stories. I practice my cough.

I am patient. I know if I wait long enough the sun will begin to set. When it finally does, we gather up our gear and trudge back through the snow.

Settled in his wagon, Andy grins hugely. "So," he says, "now what do you think of ice fishing? Great, huh?"

"Truthfully?"

"Why, sure."

"Well," I say, rubbing my numb feet in the blast of the car's heater, "I think I have finally figured out what you love about it."

Andy beams. "I knew you'd understand once you tried it."

"Right," I say. "It does feel absolutely terrific when you stop."

A SHAD IN THE DARK

"If shad were people," says Andy, "they'd hang around sleazy bars drinking beer from cans and brawling. They'd roll up their shirtsleeves so you could admire their tattoos. They'd beat up their women, who'd enjoy it. They'd never bathe and they'd belch frequently."

Because Andy's a psychiatrist, I tolerate his unusual methods of analyzing character and behavior, both fish and human. Anyway, from what I knew of the American shad, his characterization isn't far off, although before he took me to the Indianhead River, what I knew was very little.

I knew that shad roe, dipped in milk, rolled in cracker crumbs, and sauteed in butter, was a delicacy. Male shad, I surmised, were poor sources of shad roe.

I knew that spin fishermen employed shad darts to capture the fish. I suspected that the approved technique did not involve hurling small spears at them.

I knew you fished for shad in the spring, when they embarked on spawning missions up freshwater rivers from the sea.

I knew that spawning shad did not feed, but could nevertheless be enticed—or angered—into smashing artificial lures.

112

I thought I knew I wanted no part of shad fishing. I had seen the anglers lined up elbow to armpit along the banks of the Connecticut River below the Holyoke Dam, heaving heavily weighted spinning lures into turbulent water. Hooked fish appeared to fight strongly. Lines tangled regularly. Anglers cursed good-naturedly. It looked like fun—but not my kind of fun.

Not for a fly fisherman.

"*Au contraire,*" Andy told me as we wheeled through rush hour traffic heading for Boston's South Shore one glorious May afternoon a couple years ago. "We'll catch 'em on flies, all right. In a little stream that'll remind you of our Massachusetts trout rivers. You'll love it." He glanced at me meaningfully. "Libido," he whispered, as if that explained everything.

I have long suspected that Andy believes libido *does* explain everything.

"They lie in the deep holes and channels during the daytime," he explained. "On dark days, or after the sun leaves the water, they move into the shallows to spawn. They seek out tributaries of the big main rivers, like the Indianhead. Come dusk, they go absolutely bonkers. You'll see. They'll start rolling and cavorting all over the place. They'll come crashing against your legs. Totally sex-crazed. All inhibitions cast away. Aggression. Territoriality. Males and females alike. Not," he added, "that different from people, when you think about it. Shad have tons of libido."

American shad, commonly referred to as "poor man's salmon," Andy continued, are a hardier breed than our lamented Atlantic salmon, "Who," he said, "wear three-piece suits and sip martinis and only make love between clean sheets." Because the spawning needs of the shad are more flexible, they have managed to survive the polluted water and hydroelectric and flood-control projects that nearly doomed the less-adaptable salmon.

In Massachusetts, the North River, of which the Indianhead, our destination that day, is the main tributary, hosts a consistently large shad run every May. Each spring close to half a million shad run up the Connecticut River. The spawning run up the Merrimack has grown consistently over the past decade. American shad range over the entire East Coast, from the St. Johns River in Florida to the Gulf of St. Lawrence. Their spawning run, triggered by freshwater temperatures of about fifty degrees, peaks in March on the St. Johns and in May in my New England rivers. Shad were introduced into California waters in 1871 and readily established themselves on the West Coast. They are mainly concentrated in the San Francisco Bay area and in the San Joaquin and Sacramento river watersheds, although they range from San Diego to southern Alaska.

"Most people who fish for shad," said Andy, "fish the big rivers during the daytime. Heavy tackle to get down deep. You can take 'em on flies. But you need lots of weight. That's why they use all those beads. Not that much fun. But shad are surface spawners. Darkness brings them into the shallows. That's when you can take 'em on trout gear."

"What kind of flies?"

He grinned. "Bonefish flies. Just wait."

I decided not to tell him that I knew even less about bonefish than I did about shad. Bonefish roe? Bonefish darts?

Andy wheeled into the parking lot just downstream from the West Elm Street Bridge. It was a little after seven. The place was jammed—four-wheel-drives with boat racks, battered old Ford Pintos, Cadillacs, even a Porsche. I grabbed my camera and shouldered my way through a mob of hip-booted beer drinkers who were leaning on their spinning rods and watching the river. The Indianhead here ran quick and shallow between slick mud banks. It was, as Andy had said, no more than a roll cast wide.

114

I looked upstream and down and my heart sank. Fishermen were spaced out as far as I could see within easy conversation distance from each other, flipping their darts and gossiping loudly. Nobody had caught anything, I was told. Too early. Too bright. Not to worry.

I noticed that lines tangled frequently. The overhanging streamside brush was liberally festooned with garlands of monofilament and ornamental shad darts. I heard nobody complain.

I snapped some photos of the mob, just for the record, figuring that the available light would soon desert me. Then I went back to Andy's car to climb into my waders and rig up my fly rod.

"Nobody's fly fishing," I reported.

He just winked and handed me a fly.

"Bonefish fly?"

He nodded.

It didn't look like much. Tinsel body, a few strands of white bucktail, and weighted eyes on a size four or six short-shanked hook. "The eyes are the secret," said Andy. "Makes the hook ride upside-down, prevents snagging the bottom. Actually," he added, "it's just the fly-rod equivalent of a shad dart. On your 8-weight outfit with weight-forward line it'll cast fine in these close quarters."

So, armed with fly rod, flashlight, and camera, I followed Andy downstream along the riverbank. "We'll just find some elbow room," he said. "There really aren't any particular hot spots. As soon as it's dusk, the shad'll work up into this moving water to have their sex. All we're looking for is some place where we can cast." He glanced back over his shoulder at me. "Mind the mud, now. It gets slippery."

I started to remind him of the thousands of streamside miles I had trod in my angling career.

115

Instead, I said, "Whoops!" as my feet shot out from under me and I slid on my fanny into the river like an otter.

I came up spitting water. "As I was saying," said Andy.

"Just don't mention libido again."

So soaking wet and considerably humbled—but still curious—I waded out beside Andy. I imitated his style as he cast a short line three-quarters downstream. Sometimes he quickly twitched back the bonefish fly. Sometimes he held it in the downstream current, wiggling it back and forth in a more or less stationary position. Sometimes he worked it back slowly with rod tip lowered. It didn't matter. Nothing hit.

The sky darkened above us. Our awareness of the other fishermen around us faded as conversations died down. I sensed it was time to get serious. But for half an hour I saw no evidence that a single fish swam in the Indianhead.

Then came a holler from somewhere downstream. "Fish on!" A few minutes later a guy twenty yards below us called the same thing. His spinning reel shrieked and his rod bowed as he stumbled away into the darkness after his shad.

A fish sloshed near where I had cast. "I rose one," I said.

"Doubt it," said Andy. "The fish are moving up. You'll know it when you have a hit."

Suddenly, as if someone had turned on a switch, our pool was churning with shad. They rolled, swirled, and careened around. One smacked against my waders. They trailed erratic wakes like maverick torpedoes.

Then Andy tied into one. "Big fish," he grunted. This one headed upstream. "Excuse me! Fish on!" called Andy. The upstream anglers reeled in and backed away. His fish angled for streamside riprap and Andy bullied him back, his nine-foot graphite rod bent dangerously. When he netted it ten minutes later he grinned sheepishly at me. He had hooked it on the

116

back, just forward of the dorsal fin. "They'll fight like crazy, hooked that way," he said. He released the sleek four-pounder. "Happens a lot, the way these fish bang around in these close confines. It's illegal to snag shad, though some, regettably, do it. It's certainly unethical to keep one that's foul-hooked."

Moments later my fly was whacked with a blow that nearly dislocated my shoulder. For an instant I felt the powerful weight of a sea-run shad. Then he was gone.

"Tender mouths," said Andy.

"Nothing tender about the way they strike," I answered.

It grew dark. Clouds scudded past a nearly full moon. Mosquitoes descended. I wondered if Andy would attribute their appetites to libido. Shouts echoed from up and down the river. "Fish on!" "Coming through!"

Andy caught another one, this one mouth-hooked. He killed it and took it to the riverbank. "They're great eating fish," he said. "Tricky to clean, but worth it. Al McClane's book tells you how."

Then I hooked one. My shad never leaped. But he tore line off my reel in short tenacious runs. He raced from bank to bank, then took off upstream. "Fish on!" I yelled, and stumbled after him, wary of mud banks. When I finally netted him and shone my flashlight on him, I saw a silvery fork-tailed fish, deep-bellied and muscular. I added it to Andy's string.

Our shad orgy lasted for about three hours. As nearly as I could judge, Andy and I caught about as many shad on our bonefish flies as the spin casters did on their shad darts. We landed seven lip-hooked shad and released several others that we had accidentally snagged. They ranged in size from three to five pounds. Roe-laden females sometimes run as heavy as eight pounds. In the darkness around us, anglers yelled and cursed. Hooked shad ran between my legs and wrapped monofilament around my ankles. Fishermen stumbled though our pool. Boy and girl shad mated with glorious lack of inhibition.

"Libido!" shouted Andy several times. "Ain't it wonderful?"

Finally around eleven-thirty Andy announced it was time to leave. There didn't appear to be any abatement in the action, but he had an appointment at seven the next morning with a patient who, he said, had a lot in common with smallmouth bass.

BIG MOUTHS IN
SMALL PLACES

My favorite neighborhood trout brook receives its annual spring stocking at two highway bridges. These bridges are popular and convenient spots for local anglers to try their luck. They are also, not coincidentally, the places where large numbers of trout are caught.

They are places I avoid—which may account for the fact that I often fail to catch large numbers of trout.

I am a seeker of solitude. I quest for adventure, even the tame sort of adventure that might lurk a half-mile from a highway bridge. I have therefore trudged upstream from the lower bridge and downstream from the upper one, hoping to find tranquility and whatever adventure—not to mention the odd trout—that might await me between those bridges.

I have learned that trout tend to migrate very slowly from the places where they have been dumped. The fishermen who hang around bridges know what they're doing.

My upstream and downstream treks always ended at the edge of a big bog halfway between the two bridges. The brook meanders cold and deep through this godforsaken thousand acres. In

119

April it remains flooded. The streambed is difficult to locate and impossible to approach on foot. In May the water begins to recede, uncovering a daunting landscape of potholes, grassy hummocks, alder clumps, and waist-high marsh grass. Mallards build their nests in the leftover puddles. Herons fish there. Large snakes—I have been assured they are harmless, but I remain skeptical—slither underfoot. Muskrats abound. I have jumped deer there. Mosquitoes reproduce extravagantly.

Of one thing I am certain: This part of my brook is not heavily fished.

Once in May I launched my canoe from the upstream bridge and paddled and drifted downstream into the bog, armed with my new 2-weight graphite fly rod. The water looked grand, with plenty of dark undercut banks, deep eddying pools, and a few quickening riffles—just the sorts of places to which large trout might migrate in search of a haven and enough cold water to survive the heat of the summer. Surely the surrounding swale would provide abundant insect forage for them.

I caught no trout that day. May, I concluded, was still too early for them. I assumed they continued to lurk around bridge abutments stealing worms and cheese-scented marshmallows off fish hooks. I vowed to return later.

It was close to the end of June when I finally did it. I stepped into my hip boots, assembled my 2-weight, and tied on a bushy brown nymph. It was a warm, muggy day, and I was soon drenched in sweat as I slogged through the undergrowth toward the bog. Mosquitoes and blackflies found all the crevices and orifices on my body. The marsh grass had now grown to shoulder height. The puddles had mostly evaporated, leaving treacherous mud holes that were impossible to locate except by sinking into them.

But the stream looked terrific. Shaded on its borders by grass, it ran dark and cool and deep. Occasionally I saw a large cream-colored mayfly drifting on its surface. Now, surely, I thought, I would find trout.

My angling technique was simplistically primitive. Hunkering on the bank in that tall grass made fly casting impossible. So I extended the rod over the stream and let the fat nymph sink and tumble into the depths like some bug that had fallen from the marsh grass. I watched where my leader touched the surface for the telltale hesitation that meant a trout.

And on the third drift through the first pool it happened—not a dainty twitch, but a slashing strike that bowed my rod and set the hook all by itself. Nor did that trout come flopping to the surface from the pressure of the rod the way the little hatchery-reared fellows that were stocked in April usually did. This one slogged stubbornly toward the bottom, then pivoted and bulled its way upstream. Finding a rocky riffle there, it turned and showed itself for the first time in a somersaulting leap.

My trout wasn't a trout.

It was a largemouth bass.

I do not exaggerate when I report the sizes of the fish I catch. The ones that get away—maybe. In any case, after I was able to subdue this bass and heft it from the water, and before I released it, I measured it against the markings on my rod. Seventeen inches, a fat prespawn female. I didn't weigh her, but I guessed she went more than three pounds. Others, I know, would report it as four.

This on a little two-ounce rod, with a 3X tippet and a #12 brown nymph.

Had it been a trout, I would have considered it a trophy.

I was thrilled, right?

Wrong, actually. I had come to a trout brook in search of trout. I had failed.

Largemouth bass fishing to me means ponds and lakes and deer-hair bugs, the search for structure, the preoccupation with size. Bass fishing has its own aura and repertoire of techniques. In its proper place, I love fishing for largemouths.

But when I'm trout fishing, only trout will do.

I had a smoke and tried to reorder my thinking. I have caught smallmouths on trout gear in cold Maine streams. They ran universally small, and they were almost too abundant and easy to catch. Still, it's been pleasant enough. Fishing is fishing.

This was different. This, I realized, intrigued me. These were largemouths, and apparently big ones. They didn't belong. So I decided I would fish for bass. I would do it as if I were fishing for trout—with trout equipment on a trout stream. And for the rest of that afternoon I enjoyed one of the strangest and most productive largemouth bass experiences of my life. Every pool seemed to hold a bass or two. They lay tight against undercuts and deep in pools and behind submerged boulders. They lay, in other words, exactly where I would have expected trout to lie, and I fished for them the same way I would have fished for trout. They sucked in that brown nymph greedily. Several of them were as large as that first one.

It wasn't hard to deduce where the bass came from. My brook empties into a small pond notable for its bass—a place where occasional trout are taken by bass fishermen who, perhaps, are disappointed to discover they haven't caught a bass.

Since that day I have sought out other streams that are connected, however indirectly, to warmwater lakes and ponds, and in the summer I have fished them for bass, trout-style.

Often I have been rewarded with spectacular fishing. I have

taken bass in rills so narrow that I could leap over them, and sometimes they have been large bass. A friend of mine, with whom I shared this secret, claims he caught a six-pounder from such a brook.

Prospecting for new bass hideaways has given me almost as much pleasure as finding fish in them. I like to paddle the shorelines of known bass ponds, scouting for inlets. A snake-shaped break in a bed of lily pads may hint at a channel and an otherwise indiscernable incoming current. Sometimes a narrow cut in shoreside brush unveils a feeder brook. Often silt builds up at the inlet and the brook appears impassable. This, I have learned, can be deceptive. When I have paddled, poled, or dragged my canoe above the delta, I have sometimes found clear deep-running streams cutting through swamp and forest.

I have spent many happy hours scrutinizing topographic maps, reading the meandering blue strands that attach to ponds and lakes known for bass and imagining the secrets that live there. Sometimes, of course, what looks so promising on the map turns out to be a tepid, dried-up trickle, inhospitable even to the most adaptable bass. If it were foolproof, though, it wouldn't be as much fun.

Narrow shallow brooks can be deceptive, however. I found one that looked good on a map, but when I walked it up in June, it proved to be ankle-deep and mud-bottomed. It ran cooler than I expected, though, and having already invested a half-hour in getting there from the road, I followed its down-stream course. I soon came upon a dogleg where an even tinier trickle entered and a long slow pool ran dark against a high bank.

It looked trouty.

Hell. It looked bassy.

I took seven largemouths from that pool on the Panther Martin spinner I flipped with my ultralight spinning rod. I guessed that they had meandered upstream during the higher spring waters, and when the brook's depths receded toward summer they were forced to congregate, effectively trapped, in that hole. I found two other such holding pools along a one-mile stretch of otherwise barren water in that little brook. Both were likewise full of hungry bass.

Why do largemouths seek out these places? Perhaps the springtime spawning urge sends them off in search of breeding grounds. It may be that as summer approaches, the marginally cooler waters of inlets lure them from the shallow, oxygen-poor pond environment. Maybe they find easier foraging on the frogs, crawfish, baitfish, and terrestrial and aquatic insects that thrive in these brooks.

Or maybe bass, like bass fishermen, are endowed with an adventurous spirit. Wanderlust draws them up into the brooks simply because they're there. This explanation satisfies me as much as any other.

Although I am a fly fisherman by preference, I am willing to adapt my technique to the place. My little ultralight spinning rod is the weapon of choice because of its adaptability. I can flip trout-sized spinners, unweighted nightcrawlers, or flies with a bubble from my knees even when the willows and alders grow as thick as a hairbrush along the banks.

The best time to fish these places, of course, is whenever the urge strikes. I have had my best luck, though, on dark humid days—the very sorts of days when blackflies and mosquitoes bite best. Shade seems to loosen shallow-water largemouth inhibitions, so on sunny days I concentrate on the dark edges and deepest pools. I've had consistently good luck on rising water after a day or two of a summer rainstorm. Flashy spinners and drifted nightcrawlers work best under these conditions.

Toward evening largemouths in these places will sometimes surface-feed like trout, moving into current funnels to suck in whatever bugs may float through. Terrestrial trout patterns such as beetles and hoppers have worked well for me, although I suspect pattern makes less difference than stealth.

Small-brook largemouths, I have found, tend to be hungry and strong and bold. I prefer to imagine—and I think it's true—that I alone know where these fish live, and that I am the only one who fishes for them. The secrecy, the delicious taste of discovery, the conviction that no one else fishes in these places, all spice the thrill of the quick tug and the cart-wheeling leap of a surprised bass.

There have been times, naturally, when bass fishing in these little trickles has disappointed me.

On those days, the only thing I could catch was a bunch of trout.

Part 5
ROD ENVY

It's a very old photo, crinkled and rust-colored, and it shows me clutching, in one hand, a very long fly rod, and in the other I'm holding a line from the end of which dangles a very small sunfish. I'm wearing shorts held up by suspenders. My hair is curly and fair. I appear to be about two years old. This photo, I am told, records my first rod-and-reel fish, although it's possible that someone else hooked it for me and my contribution was to derrick it in.

That sunfish is not my first fishing memory. I don't remember it all.

My father fished avidly. Family vacations were fishing vacations. I spent most of my young summers trolling from boats while my peers were playing sandlot baseball. This, I believe, accounts for my failure to make it to the big leagues.

But I have no specific memories of those times, either, although Dad assures me that I was catching landlocked salmon and smallmouth bass from Maine lakes before I could recite the alphabet.

My first concrete angling recollection is of my first rod. It was a willow switch that Dad cut for me from the swamp in back of our house. I vaguely understood that he and I were sharing some sort of rite, although its significance was lost on me at the time.

Dad owned several dozen fishing rods, and I didn't understand why he wouldn't just give one of them to me. I knew it wasn't that he valued them too highly to entrust to the hands of a child. He gave away his rods to friends and casual acquaintances about as fast as he acquired them, and in later years he allowed me to bust the tips of plenty of his fine split-bamboo fly rods.

He could have given me one of his rods. But I had to have a willow switch. He rejected several saplings before he found the right one. He cut it down and waved it back and forth, commenting on its flexibility and taper, weight and length. He peeled off its bark, then rigged it with butcher's twine. His only shortcut was to tie on a real hook.

I used it once. I found it inefficient. Dad relented and gave me a bamboo fly rod and a Pflueger Medalist reel with double-tapered line, instantly making me the best-equipped six-year-old fisherman in town. I discarded the willow switch, along with whatever lessons Dad had hoped I would learn from participating in its creation and fishing with it. I was too interested in catching fish.

Before long, I was practicing plug casting in the back yard with my own steel bait-casting rod. When spinning rods became popular, Dad gave me one of them. A couple years later he gave me an ultralight outfit, imported from Italy. I owned several fly rods—one for trout, one for bass, and one for roll-casting worms into the tepid suburban ponds near my house.

One of my friends, whose father flew airplanes and thought

fishing was useless, bought himself a telescoping steel rod. Despite all my gear, this was the rod I wanted. Since Dad didn't have one for me, and thought they were inefficient instruments anyway, I bought one with my allowance money. It worked poorly, as Dad had predicted, so I abandoned it for bamboo.

When fiberglass came along, Dad's rod collection quickly doubled. The rows of aluminum tubes holding the bamboo rods gathered dust. The glass ones worked better.

When I made my first trip to the West, I brought along a lovely little seven-and-a-half-foot, two-ounce glass rod. I quickly learned that my equipment pegged me as a novice. Everybody who took his fishing seriously used graphite. Every fisherman I ran into in the West—most of whom were easterners—owned a graphite dry-fly rod, a graphite nymph rod, and a graphite streamer rod. Plus spares of each. And not just graphite. Sage graphite, or Winston or Loomis or Fenwick or Orvis or Scott. Loomis was especially big that summer.

I learned that the rod revealed the fisherman. Everybody had his opinion. Sage men sneered at Orvis men. And vice versa. High modulus was a good thing. Ditto boron. I didn't understand much of it. All I knew was that my little fiberglass rod had done irreparable damage to my stature. It had nothing whatsoever to do with how accurately or far I could cast with it (I could hold my own with most of them), or how many large trout I caught (many, in fact). Nobody who used fiberglass on the Railroad Ranch or the Madison River could be taken seriously. The trout I caught with that rod were an affront to good angling taste.

When I got home, I bought a Loomis. Who wouldn't? The following summer out West I discovered that Loomis had dropped several notches in the ranks of the conventional wisdom. It started me thinking, and I remembered my first rod, that willow switch. Then, finally, I got my first glimmer of Dad's thinking. "First principles, son," I think he was saying. "Don't lose track of where it starts and what it's all about."

Well, I've stuck with the Loomis, and I still use that little glass rod occasionally. Still, I keep hearing that truly serious anglers nowadays prefer antique bamboo rods, and the rod builders currently most admired craft wonderfully expensive reproductions from Tonkin cane.

One day I expect we'll swing back to first principles such as willow switches. I hope so. I figure I finally know all about them.

THE *NEWSWEEK* PAPERS

In the April 10, 1989 issue of *Newsweek* magazine, the following words appeared:

In Defense of Outdoorsmen

by

William G. Tapply

Last year I bought fishing licenses in Massachusetts, Maine, New Hampshire, Connecticut, Montana, Idaho, and Colorado. I caught trout in all those states. Hundreds of trout. Some of them were quite large. I returned every one of them to the river. My friends who don't fish think this is crazy. "Don't you like to eat trout?" they ask.

They shake their heads. They don't get it.

I also hunt. I shoot at ducks and ruffed grouse and woodcock with my shotgun. Sometimes—not very often, but sometimes—I hit what I am aiming at. I do not put back the birds I kill. I wish I could. But the fact that I can't doesn't stop me. This is equally incomprehensible to the same friends. "How can you kill beautiful wild creatures?" they ask.

131

They find my attitude inconsistent. That's okay. I think theirs is, too.

I've tried to explain the lure of the outdoors to my friends. How fields of frosted goldenrod crunch underfoot, how a fly line loops toward the ring of a trout's rise, how a setter on point quivers and whines, how bullfrogs burp, woodcock whistle, and ruffed grouse drum, how the scent of Hoppes gun oil and wet bird dogs and discharged shotgun shells conjure up earlier times with my dad and Burt Spiller and others who hunt no longer, how . . .

But the parts do not make the whole.

We hook-and-bullet types are doomed to be misunderstood. We are simultaneously viewed as quixotic poets and seething sadists. The worst of it is that we are not regarded as reliable witnesses on environmental concerns. We have axes to grind— as if nobody else did.

Jefferson, in a letter to Madison in 1789, said, "The earth belongs in usufruct to the living." The key word is "usufruct." It means, according to the *American Heritage Dictionary*, "The right to utilize and enjoy the profits and advantages of something belonging to another so long as the property is not damaged or altered in any way." It's a concept most outdoorsmen understand. It's why we put back our trout.

The destruction of natural habitat is a far more insidious enemy of wildlife than sportsmen. Yes, we may kill an occasional creature, but wild creatures are renewable resources, provided the environment that nurtures them remains. That's why we lobby for reduced bag limits, stricter enforcement of regulations, preservation of marshland and wilderness, protection of endangered species.

Sadly, we are largely ignored. We are lumped with crazy people who shoot high-powered rifles at cows and automobiles. We lack votes. So instead, wetlands are drained and excavated and condoed, woodlands are bulldozed and paved and super-marketed, trout streams are straightened and dredged and diverted through concrete culverts, and sportsmen are outlobbied by commercial fishermen. If this were the worst of it, I suppose I would accept it with sad resignation. But this, in fact, is the least of it.

Our oceans have become the world's cesspools. The earth's atmosphere fights a losing battle against the poisons we spew into it. Acid spills from the sky. Deadly radiation slips through holes in our ozone layer. Polar ice caps melt inexorably. No one knows what to do with toxic or nuclear waste. South American forests disappear, and with them nature's great balancing act of photosynthesis.

When I was young, I took the purity and natural beauty of the places I fished and hunted for granted. Now I have become resigned to their corruption. I also used to accept without question that the air I breathed, the water I drank, and the food I ate would not kill me or my children.

I actually believed that a presidential campaign would popularize the issues. I actually believed the candidates would vie with each other to see who could utter the most extravagant promises for our environment. It's not that I place great faith in election-year promises. I don't. But a promise, at least, would be an acknowledgement. I heard no promises. What hope is there for an issue that doesn't even deserve an election-year promise?

I had hope for George Bush. He called himself an outdoorsman, the "environmental president." I saw photos of him fishing, hunting, camping. But he chose to frame the environmental debate with a snide swipe at his opponent's failure to clean up the harbor in Boston. The governor puffed that it wasn't his fault, and that was that. The environment wasn't a sexy issue. There weren't many votes there. Boston Harbor was to the environment what Willie Horton was to law and order— a cartoon.

We are told that the cost of rescuing our environment must be measured against the profits of industries, that the importance of cleaning up our mess should be balanced against the interests of those who create the mess, and that if the government will just continue to finance studies it will be demonstrating ample commitment—especially if studies can be funded without raising taxes. Those of us who expect more are labeled extremists, environmental nuts. Our cries are called polemics. We are, at best, nuisances. At most, we should be appeased.

Outdoorsmen have witnessed firsthand the murder of rivers where Atlantic salmon used to spawn. We have seen sterile mountain lakes and stands of dead wilderness timber where trout once swam and birds and animals once thrived. Heath hens and passenger pigeons and scores of other creatures are extinct. The list of endangered species grows every year. These realities were once abstractions.

Hunters and fishermen know.

And we despair.

"I'm shocked," wrote L. A. of West Vancouver, B. C. to the *Newsweek* editor, "that a magazine of *Newsweek*'s calibre would print this type of hypocritical crap."

"I was shocked at the logical inconsistencies in the article," said S. S. of Los Angeles, while M. P. of New York City added, "What arrogance!" "Totally absurd," concurred D. L. of Newton Square, Pennsylvania. "Trivial," was the word of D. L. of Hopedale, Massachusetts. "I had to stifle my laughter," said F.

M., a veterinarian from Tarzana, California. F. R. of Sun Valley, Nevada, added, "Bah! Phooey!"

"Pathetic and paradoxical," wrote B. M. of Southington, Connecticut, noting that the author "fails to capture the moment when a beautiful bird in flight explodes in a shower of blood, intestines, and feathers." In the same vein, V. W. of Miami said, "I am sure that as a shot guns [sic] blast rips him from the sky the duck who falls earthward feels great contentment in knowing his existence has just been ended by an environmentalist who wishes he could put back the birds he kills."

"The most stupid piece ever printed by *Newsweek*," penned J. S. of Palm Desert, California. "Made me want to puke . . . Mr. Tapply is a vicious, small boy in a 48 year old body. Shame!"

R. A. of Quincy, Massachusetts, wrote to me of his concern for "the hungry fish you terrorize," and T. H. from New York City pointed out that the writer "has contributed to these problems by losing lead sinkers from his fishing lines." K. S. of Spanaway, Washington, added, "I'm sure the trout he releases don't feel the 'sport' to be quite as benign as all that. But of course I wouldn't know, not being a trout."

T. G., on the stationery of an organization called People for the Ethical Treatment of Animals, in Washington, D.C., wrote, "It isn't surprising that William Tapply is a fiction writer . . . maybe . . . he's forgotten how to write a factual article." W. P. of Boston, speaking for The Fund for Animals, pointed out that hunters "shot and killed more than 200 million wild animals" in 1987 (50 million mourning doves, 25 million quail, 12 million ducks, 27 million squirrels, 20,000 black bears, 1,500 mountain lions, among others). "I'd hate to see the body count if they killed wild animals frequently, rather than just occasionally," he added. And T. M. of the Animal Protection Institute of America, while conceding that "William G. Tapply writes well," cautioned, "But don't you be fooled, America."

Oh, well.

I received nearly a hundred letters. About half of them liked the piece.

"Well written, poignant, and timely," wrote D. S. of Independence, Missouri. "Eloquent," was the word of J. E. of Bessemer, Michigan, and M. R., a ninth grader from Maxwell, New Mexico, said, "I am glad that *Newsweek* had the guts to come out and print this article."

And so on.

The folks whose views I mirrored in the article liked it. Those who didn't understand hunting and fishing before they read it continued not to.

The response was, all in all, depressing. Clearly I failed to change a single mind or to move an opinion even one degree.

The article was *not* intended to defend outdoorsmen. The title was supplied by *Newsweek*. My purpose was to call attention to the condition of our natural world. Every letter writer very obviously shared my concern. My piece, nevertheless, was a red flag for half of them.

It was no consolation to learn just how accurate my perceptions were. Those who don't hunt and fish did, indeed, find my attitudes "inconsistent." They seemed to believe I am a "seething sadist" and surely not a "reliable witness on environmental concerns." Obviously, I have "axes to grind."

My suspicions were confirmed. My despair was deepened.

I answered, individually and laboriously, the first batch of letters that were forwarded to me from *Newsweek*. I turned the other cheek to my critics. I elaborated on views I thought I had stated clearly in the article. I thanked those who praised the piece, urging them to fight the good fight.

Finally, I gave up. I didn't have the time, energy, or patience for it. It was all too depressing. Anyway, it became clear that the pen, or at least mine, isn't all that mighty.

Now I have composed a generic letter of reply to all those who took the time to write to me. I have no hope whatsoever that it will prompt anybody to think, but here it is anyway:

Dear Correspondent:

I apologize for not answering your thoughtful letter personally. The "My Turn" article in *Newsweek* elicited about a hundred responses.

To those of you whose views are similar to mine, you must know, as I have learned, that we continue to be misunderstood by a depressingly large number of our fellow citizens. It will take more than an article such as mine to persuade them to rethink their position. They persist in believing that hunting and fishing is evil and that those of us who do it must be sadistic. It surprised me to learn that most environmentalists consider outdoorspeople (hunters and fishermen) their enemies.

What can we do? We must try to build bridges to those who care about the outdoors but who can't—or don't want to—understand us. The environment is everybody's concern. Otherwise, I fear that we will squander our energies sniping at each other's differences. We hunters and fishermen are equally guilty. Some of us sneer at those who equate the death of a wild creature with the murder of a human being. We call them "bleeding hearts," or worse. We mock their hypocrisy for eating the flesh of animals, poultry, or fish. We ask them if they believe living organisms such as onions and apples have immortal, anthropomorphic souls, as they seem to think birds and fish do. We bristle when they attack our sport. We bridle at their close-mindedness.

137

One thing we can do is join and contribute money to their organizations. Write for their newsletters. Attend their meetings. Let them get to know us—to see that we aren't sadists at all, that we're on the same side of the important issues.

We must make our critics understand that our differences are far outweighed by what we share. If we're to have any hope in accomplishing this, we must behave ourselves and police ourselves. There are lots of people who fish and hunt who don't deserve to be called "sportsmen" or "outdoorsmen."

To my critics—those of you who called my article "crap" and worse, who lectured me on the meaning of life and the world "usufruct," who called me a sadist and a hypocrite—I plead guilty of failing to express myself better.

My article was not intended to defend outdoorsmen in the first place. Naively, it hadn't occurred to me that we needed the defending we evidently do. "In Defense of Outdoorsmen" was the title the magazine editors, not I, gave the piece. I wanted only to plead for our world before, as I felt then (and feel even more profoundly now after hearing from you), it's too late. Please—we are natural allies, whether or not you approve of hunting and fishing. All of you care about the natural world. So do we outdoorsmen. Honestly.

All of you who wrote in response to my article share this with each other and with me: You care. That's what's important. What can we do about it?

Sincerely yours,

William G. Tapply

A GUY I KNOW

I have a friend—well, he's more than a friend—actually, less than a friend, too—I'll try to explain—anyway, he lives to fish, and I like the way he thinks. I wish you could meet him.

His name is Brady Coyne. He's a lawyer, a bachelor, and he lives alone in an apartment on the Boston waterfront. His place is cluttered with old *Field & Stream* magazines, Metz hackle necks, and waders that need patching. He works in a tall office building in Copley Square. On Fridays during the season he hangs a "Gone Fishin'" sign on his door, to the consternation of Julie, his secretary.

During the off months when he's supposed to be working he spends too much time swiveled around with his back to his desk gazing through the city smog and over the rooftops westward, in the direction of his Massachusetts rivers, the Swift and the Deerfield, and in his imagination he sees farther—to the Bighorn and the Madison and the Henry's Fork.

On winter weekends he listens to the basketball game while he ties flies.

Brady doesn't love his work. He loves fishing. His work is a means toward an end. His end is to fish every trout river in the world.

I don't know about you, but I can appreciate a guy like Brady. We have a lot in common. I even envy him a bit.

Here's the way he tries to explain himself:

For most of my clients, most of the time, the ability to chat with a lawyer about hypothetical problems is worth a lot of money. For me, being available to chat with wealthy clients about imaginary legal issues is my work, for which I am rewarded with handsome retainers. Sometimes real problems appear. Usually they don't. People—especially very rich people—get nervous when they don't have problems. Not having a problem becomes a problem. My peculiar legal specialty is helping wealthy old people feel comfortable about not having problems.

I rarely am asked to write articles for learned journals about my specialty.

Sometimes my clients actually do get divorced or arrested. Sometimes they decide to buy a new business, or sell an old one. They set up trusts for children and grandchildren. They look for tax dodges. Eventually, they die. All of these activities require planning, consulting, conferring. Options need to be studied. Game plans must be drawn up.

It keeps me busy.

It does not preoccupy me.

My friends marvel at my law practice. How easy it is, how lucrative.

How boring.

They usually seem envious.

I explain to them that I fish for trout. Often and avidly. Fishing, I tell my friends, is a great deal like sex. When it's good, it's absolutely wonderful. And when it's bad, it's still pretty damn good.

In fast-moving parts of eastern rivers, small trout lie in shallow riffles. They feed eagerly. They strike willingly at almost any sort of artificial fly that floats near them. Sometimes, I tell my friends, I will cast to these fish. They pose no particular challenge. I never doubt that I will catch several of them.

Fishing for them keeps me busy.

It does not preoccupy me.

I am also acquainted, I tell my friends, with a large brown trout who lives in a slow-moving stretch of the lower Swift River. He lies behind a sunken log up against a steep bank that is overhung by birch trees whose branches nearly brush the surface of the water. My brown trout feeds on the small insects that get trapped in the sluggish eddy where it is impossible to make a dry fly float in a natural manner. He weighs at least four pounds, and I would like to persuade him to strike at my fly.

I like to sit on the bank and smoke and ponder the problem. What fly might that old brown trout take? How can I cast it without spooking him? Should I wait until evening? Perhaps come at night, or before sunrise in the morning, to fish for him?

So far, I haven't actually cast toward that brown trout. I figure I'm going to get one chance. I want to make sure I've thought it through.

It's a problem of tactics and execution that I have not yet resolved.

This brown trout does preoccupy me.

Occasionally, my law practice brings me the equivalent of that Swift River brown trout, a difficult case, a challenge, a situation unprecedented in my experience that requires me, metaphorically, to negotiate overhanging branches, deceptive, swirling currents, and a shrewd, experienced adversary. The death of Maggie Winter struck me as one of those. . . .

141

Rod Envy

I forgot to mention that Brady's clients, being wealthy, are sometimes victimized by criminals. Occasionally one of these clients, or one of their relatives, gets murdered. When this happens, Brady tends to find himself wandering around in the middle of a murder case.

He'd rather be fishing, though. A couple years ago, for example, he had to go to Vermont on such a case. He had a pretty girl with him (that's one of the differences between Brady and me) and it was inevitable that he would find a trout stream where he and his lady friend could have a picnic:

When I finished eating I stood up, brushed the crumbs off the front of my shirt, and walked the few feet to the steep edge where a rocky ledge sloped directly down to the stream. A little pine-needled shelf jutted out over a deep, green pool where the currents funneled against the ledge. I lay down on my belly, propped my chin in my hands, and peered down into the water.

The pool was dappled in filtered sunlight. I could see straight down through the martini-clear water. I could count the rocks and pebbles on the bottom. It took me a few minutes to find what I was looking for.

Allowing for refraction, I guessed he was fourteen or fifteen inches long. He lay as still as a waterlogged stick behind a small boulder near the head of the pool, a grey ghostly shape. His body and tail waved rhythmically with the currents. As I watched, he seemed to float upward toward the surface. He drifted backward a few feet, his nose nearly touching the buff-colored mayfly that floated above. Then with a suddenness that belied his otherwise effortless motions, he raised his snout out of the water and gave a quick powerful twist of his tail that left a tiny whirlpool where he had been. The mayfly had disappeared. My trout sank back into the water and casually finned to his post behind the boulder.

A moment later the trout repeated the performance, and again, and I learned his feeding rhythm, and I knew that if I waded across the river downstream of this pool, where shallow water bubbled over a rocky riffle, and crept up the far bank, crouched low to present no silhouette, and took up a position fifteen feet down and to the side of that trout, and if I cast carefully four or five feet upstream of his lie, with a little right-hand curve in the leader, and if I had managed to tie on the right fly, and if the leader tippet wasn't too coarse, and if I mended my line properly so that the artificial would float naturally down to him at the instant when he was ready to eat again—if I did all that, perhaps this fish would drift under my fly and lift up his snout and flick his tail and suck it in. And if I was alert, I would raise my rod tip firmly and I would drive the tiny hook into his jaw, and if I gentled him just right I might lead him to my net. Then I would cradle him in my hand and twist the hook from his jaw and lower him into the river. I'd hold him there with his nose pointed into the current until I was sure that his gills were pulsing. Then I'd take my hand away and he'd pause for a moment, suspended at my feet, until he realized he was free. He'd flick his tail and dart back to his position behind his boulder.

Soon he'd forget what had happened to him. Fifteen minutes later he'd begin feeding again. But then if I cast my fly to him, something primeval would flash in the tiny bit of matter that passed as his brain, and he would not follow it. Maybe tomorrow, but not again today.

"What is it?"

I jerked my head around. "Jesus, Kat. Please don't ever sneak up on me like that again."

143

She settled onto the ground beside me, her hip and thigh touching mine. I could feel the warmth of her along my leg. She leaned her head against my shoulder. "I'm sorry."

"It's okay. You just startled me, that's all."

"That's not what I meant. I've been a terrible grouch."

"I guess you're entitled."

"No reason to take it out on you."

"That's what lawyers are for."

"Oh, Christ . . . What're you looking at?"

"Down there. There's a nice trout. I've been watching him feed."

She hitched closer to me. "Where? I don't see any fish."

I pointed. "See that boulder?"

She put her face alongside my arm to peer down the length of it. "Yeah, I guess so."

"See behind it? There's a grey shape?"

"Mmm."

"Watch it."

An instant later the grey shape lifted, drifted, and swirled below us. "Hey!" yelled Kat. "Oh, wow! Why don't you go catch him?"

I turned to look at her. "I already did."

"Huh? When?"

"In my mind. Almost as good."

"I don't get it," she said. "Fishing, I mean. You don't even eat them. So why do it?"

"Fishing," I said, "is just the most fun a man can have standing up."

A Cape Cod kettle pond at dusk, a pretty woman paddling the canoe, trout rising, a fly rod in hand—the rascal's got it made, sometimes.

144

Brady had a lot of things on his mind that summer. But while he was fishing, nothing else mattered much.

It works that way for me, too:

A furry blanket of mist skimmed the inky surface of the pond. An orange wedge of moon hung low in the eastern sky, and toward the western horizon the brilliant gold of an hour earlier had faded to yellowish pewter. Aside from the close-up hum and zizz of swarming mosquitoes and the rhythmic distant swish of the traffic on Route 6, out there in the canoe Lily and I seemed cocooned in the liquid silence of the evening.

She had been right about the trout. The rings of surface-feeding fish caught wiggly reflections from the night sky, expanded them outward, broke the fragile light into pieces, and scattered them until they seemed to sink into the depths of the pond. They were fat healthy rainbows, averaging a foot or so in length, and they sucked in the little white-winged dry fly I cast to their swirls.

I released the first few I caught without boating them by tracing the leader down to the fly in their mouths with my fingers and twisting the tiny hook free. Finally, Lily said, "Hey, that could be our breakfast," so I lifted the next two into the canoe and snapped their necks.

She had changed into snug-fitting white jeans and a rust-colored flannel shirt. She had the sleeves rolled up to her elbows and had left several buttons on the front undone. She was adept with the paddle, although once she had pushed us up into the cove across the pond she barely had to paddle at all. Down there in the bowl formed by the hills on all sides there was no breeze to ruffle the surface of the water, and we drifted slowly on unfelt currents of moving air, just fast enough to give me new fish to cast to.

145

We hardly spoke. When we did, it was in whispers. "See that one over there?" she'd say, or, "Damn. Missed him," from me. The quiet of the place commanded respect.

There was a hypnotic rhythm to it—false-cast once, twice, shoot out the line, watch it settle like a silvery snake onto the black skin of the water, squint at the barely visible white wings of the little fly, twitch it once, pause, then the swirl, the lift of the rod tip, the pulse at the end of the line, a leap or two, quick bursts of silver light against the darkness, then the thrumming resistance as I stripped in the line with a rainbow trout hooked on the end of it.

I sat up in the bow, my back to Lily, surrounded by the place, my head empty of all else, intent only on the fishing and the silence and the pond. No thoughts of Jeff, being kept alive by machines in Hyannis, of myself, waking up with an elbow digging into my chest and a knife at my throat, of stolen Mayan jaguars, road pizzas, murdered watchdogs. In that canoe it was mindlessly sensual, and I was cleansed and filled and satisfied with the delicate organic smell of night air and water and coolness, the sounds of tiny wavelets slapping against the sides of the aluminum canoe, the feel of the dampness of the air as it gathered into droplets in the hairs on my arms, the silhouettes of shadowy night birds and bats swooping and darting over the pond and now and then brushing its skin with their wing tips.

Brady and I have a great deal in common. Many of our friends, in fact, get the two of us confused. We are, of course, quite different in many respects. But when he was talking about his day of solitary fishing in the wilderness of Maine, it reminded me of all the times I have done the same thing, and thought the same thoughts, and felt all the good feelings:

*

I shoved off from the sand beach, kneeling on the bottom of the canoe behind the middle thwart. For the first few hundred yards it was work, stroking with the paddle and feathering in the J stroke. The backs of my thighs burned, and I felt hard painful knots on the fronts of my shoulders. But gradually I found my rhythm—stroke, feather, glide. The canoe knifed through the glassy water. The only sound was the faint hiss up at the bow where the canoe sliced through the water. I was in no particular hurry. The fish would be there, and the old Indian burial ground, which I wanted to see, wasn't going anywhere. But I wanted to go fast, to step up the beat, so I could feel the air move across my face and savor that sense of power as the blade of the paddle pushed against the solidness of the lake.

I stopped paddling to glide up on a pair of mergansers that were diving and frolicking in the shallow water against the shore ahead of me. They let me approach almost into shotgun range before they dipped under the water and out of sight, and I wondered how they had become educated. Farther on, I saw a heavy swirl break the smooth surface of the lake. It could have been a bass, but I preferred to think it was a salmon. I unlimbered my fly rod and cast to it, but he didn't take. And I didn't actually care.

By the time I arrived at the mouth of Harley's Creek, I had worked up a healthy sweat. I nosed the canoe into the slow current and pushed against it. Soon I entered the channel where it cut through the big evergreen forest. The current flowed smoothly near the mouth of the river, where it narrowed before entering the lake. Then the river widened as the riverbed grew shallower, and the water bumped and eddied unevenly as it passed over submerged boulders.

147

Rod Envy

I beached the canoe and pulled on the waders I had stowed up in the bow. I tied on a bushy Royal Coachman and waded into the riffles. The little Orvis rod was a wand in my hand. The currents surged around my knees. The gaudy dry fly bobbed and drifted, and then there was a quick burst of silver. I struck too late, and felt just a momentary tug before the fly came free. I cursed, but not with enthusiasm. I felt too good on this day to care very much about failing to hook a trout. I false-cast a couple of times to dry out the fly, and then set it down as soft as an autumn leaf on the water where it divided on an exposed rock. Again, the silvery flash of a trout. This time I didn't miss him. The brook trout tugged upstream, a poor tactic, since he had to battle both the tension of my rod and the force of the moving water. Soon he allowed me to lead him down to where I stood in the water. I ran my fingers along the leader and carefully twisted the hook from his jaw.

I caught half a dozen foot-long brook trout without moving from that spot, brilliantly colored little bundles of muscle, with spots like drops of fresh blood on their flanks and flashes of orange like Baltimore orioles. Then I waded ashore and sat beside the canoe. When I lit a cigarette, I realized it was the first one I had had since breakfast. I held it in my fingers for a moment, staring at it. Then I scooped out a hole in the earth and crammed the butt into it. I stood up and ground it under my heel. I felt exhilaratingly virtuous.

I got back into the canoe and navigated the riffles, sticking to the light currents against the shore. Up ahead lay a broad, shallow stretch studded with rocks. I clambered out and, still in my waders, dragged the canoe upstream to the next pool. At that point the character of the stream became consistent: broad, deep pools alternating with shallow rapids. I didn't stop to fish. I knew that somewhere deeper into the woods the creek divided, and at the top of the bluff was the Indian burial ground. I wanted to see it. Perhaps I'd fish some more on the way back to camp.

So I paddled through the pools and dragged over the rapids, and by the time I arrived at the fork I found myself regretting my indulgences in Winstons and Jack Daniels and renewing my resolve to amend my self-destructive habits. I beached the canoe and then dragged it entirely out of the water. It was only about eleven in the morning, but I was ready for the lunch that I had hastily assembled in Bud Turner's kitchen after breakfast. It consisted of half a dozen leftover breakfast sausages, a slab of Vermont cheddar, half a loaf of home-baked bread, and a canteen of icy lake water.

I munched on my cold lunch and watched a trout that was rising steadily against the opposite bank. A kingfisher swooped over the river, dived, missed, and flew up into a tree, chattering like an out-of-tune lawn mower. After lunch I shook a Winston out of the pack. I hesitated only an instant before I put it back. I didn't need it, I told myself.

Brady fishes many of the rivers that I like. One of his favorites is also one of mine—the Deerfield, in the western part of the state where we both live.

He also suffers, like me, from a depth wish:

The section of Route 2 that runs due west across the Connecticut Valley into the mountains is called the Mohawk Trail. It's a winding two-lane highway that climbs the hills and cuts through the valleys, past old paper mills and working farms, through worn-out little villages like Erving and Turner's Falls.

149

After it crosses the Connecticut River it rises into the Berkshires and picks up the Deerfield River, which it parallels for several miles. The Deerfield is a classic trout river, big by Massachusetts standards, deep and swift, its waters kept frigid year-round by the hydroelectric dams that feed it. It boils around the great boulders that are scattered in its bed, and the trout like to lie in the eddies and suck in the insects that are funneled to them.

I stopped in Charlemont and carried my two peanut butter sandwiches to the bank of the river. I sat with my back against the trunk of an old oak. The water was high, surging over the tops of the boulders that normally lay exposed. That meant the Fife Brook Dam, a few miles upstream from where I sat, was releasing water into the river. Those of us who fished the Deerfield for trout did so cautiously, because we knew that when they let water go from the bottom of the dam, the level could rise two or three feet in a matter of minutes. We learned to listen for changes in the pitch of the water's melody. It comes rumbling, like a distant train, and it warns us to get off the river fast.

As I munched my sandwiches and watched the river rush by, I remembered the one time I had failed to heed the warning. It was near sunset of a June evening several years earlier. I was wading the Yankee Flats, only a few hundred yards downstream from the dam. Charlie McDevitt was working a pool a little downstream from me and around the bend. Down in that deep gorge where the river flowed, the sun had not touched the water for hours. It had already become too dark to tie on a new fly, so I heard the rising trout before I was able to see him. *Glug*, it went. A big fish swirling at the surface, sucking in insects, a solid, heavy, no-nonsense noise. I'd heard such sounds before, and this one made my pulse race as I remembered the size of the other fish. It was no ordinary trout. I imagined one of the eight- or ten-pound brown trout I knew fishermen occasionally took from the river—fish as long as a man's arm.

I flicked the dry fly with a couple of false casts, then with a strong thrust of wrist and forearm I cast toward the place where the fish had risen. The fly fell short. I stripped more line from the reel and cast again, striving to combine just the right proportions of delicate timing and sheer strength necessary to cast long distances with a fly rod. But I was still short. I needed to get a little closer to the fish.

I reached with my left foot, probing with my toe for the river bottom. I already stood waist-deep, and I knew somewhere ahead of me the river bottom dropped off abruptly, but I was still surprised when my foot came down nearly a foot deeper than where I had been standing. I remained there, poised, left foot ahead of right, with most of my weight still on my rear foot. Slowly I shifted my weight and edged my right foot forward beside my left. Later I remembered hearing the grumble of heavy water moving toward me, but at the time my brain was focused on the big trout and the warning didn't register.

The rising water arrived at the moment my right toe struck against a submerged rock. I felt my upper body begin to fall forward. My left foot slid sideways on the slippery gravel on the riverbed. My right foot bumped the boulder again, and in that instant of imbalance the full force of the rising river struck me at the waist, hip, and knee. I waved my arms awkwardly, seeking equilibrium, my fly rod a useless balancing staff. My body twisted so that I found myself facing directly upstream. The top half of my body began to topple backwards so that it seemed I would end up lying on the water, my face to the dark sky overhead, and shoot downstream head-first.

151

I struggled to remain upright. My feet bounced on the bottom as the growing force of the water began to carry me downstream. Water roared around my shoulders and splashed against my face. Then I went under. My mouth and nose filled, and I felt a surge of panic. I found myself twisted around facing downstream, out of control, the river surging against my shoulders. I strained to find the bottom with my toes. The dark riverbank seemed to race past. It appeared to be so close that I thought I could touch it, grab a root, hang on, and I tried to maneuver toward it. But I could reach nothing. My toes kept scraping river bottom, but I couldn't stop. My waders filled with water, pulling me down. My legs grew heavy. I thrust my head back in an effort to keep my face above water. I went under again, and the roar of water filled my ears. Avoid tipping over, I thought. Remain upright. Above all, don't tip. Then I would be totally at the whim of the river. Then I'd tumble against the bottom. I'd lose track of where the top was. I'd be crushed against underwater rocks.

I bobbed downstream, moving faster and faster, still instinctively gripping my fly rod. Sometimes I'd touch bottom with one of my feet, but then the river would pick me up and sweep me along. I willed the panic from my brain. I dropped my rod and tried to use both arms to maintain my balance by laying them flat on the surface and finning. I found I could steer a little and keep my head up that way. I tried to move away from the middle of the river, hoping to find shallower, less swift water. I kept circling and probing with my feet, reaching for the bottom. But my waders had filled, and the weight of the water in them seemed to pull me lower and lower into the river. My arms were underwater. I treaded desperately. My heavy legs moved reluctantly. The water felt as thick as mud around them. I tipped my head back to breathe. I was spinning, now facing upstream, now twisted around by the relentless force of the water. Two, three times my head went under. My toes reached nothing. I had lost the river bottom.

Suddenly, with the force of a speeding automobile colliding with a tree, I felt myself smash against a boulder. A white flash of pain surged across my hip and shoulder. I clawed frantically at the rock, but the river yanked me away. Then I was tumbling. I could no longer distinguish the surface of the river from its bottom. I bounced, shoulder and knee and head scraping and banging against gravel and rock. I was a wet rag in the mouth of a bull mastiff, at the complete mercy of the driving power of the river.

I groped wildly with my hands for the river bottom that raced under me. With a desperate heave I pushed myself upward. My head broke the surface, and I gulped a breath of sweet air before I was wrenched under again. Then something hammered the side of my head. A great sinking blackness sucked away the last of my strength.

Brady survived, of course. His partner, Charlie McDevitt, fished him out. Charlie rescued Brady's rod, too. Brady still goes back to the Deerfield. He can't forget the *Glug* that trout made in the darkness . . .

Well, I told you I'd explain. Brady's more than my friend— and less, too—I said.

Several years ago I began to write mystery novels. That's when Brady entered my life.

I invented him.

I realized I couldn't understand him very well unless he was a fisherman. This, I suppose, is a shortcoming of mine.

Fishing, and dreaming about fishing, gives Brady something

to do while other things are going on. Lots of things go on more or less at the same time in mystery novels.

Fishing defines Brady, the same way it does you and me. It focuses our values. It gives us a way of viewing the world and where we belong in it.

Like us, Brady is the kind of guy who will scorn treacherous rivers and foul weather and blackflies and leaky waders to cast to that particular trout that has challenged him. And then, like us, if he manages to catch it, he'll release it. Only those of us who do such things can understand people like us.

For Brady, fishing is a metaphor for life.

I've been working on a new novel recently. Brady's been whispering something new into my ear.

Life, he keeps insisting, is a metaphor for fishing.

I'm not sure I understand. I expect he'll eventually explain it to me. When he does, I'll pass it along to you.

MEMORY JOGGING

Last week my eight-year-old son caught his first trout.

It was a humid August afternoon, a day—like many days—good for nothing much except fishing. It was my idea. He shrugged. Why not? Eight-year-olds must pass through an inevitable shrugging stage, I have learned.

We launched my Grumman at the sand beach of Warner's Pond. Mike climbed into the bow, armed with his brand-new spin-casting outfit, a foolproof rig designed to guarantee positive reinforcement for the novice angler, a well-conceived gift from Grampa.

I paddled along the lily-padded shoreline and Mike quickly got the hang of flipping out a little Mepps spinner. Within a few minutes a bluegill the size of his palm latched onto it. Mike reeled it up to the rod tip, craned it into the canoe, and nearly capsized us when he pounced on it.

"Nice goin'," I said.

Grin. Shrug.

We completed a half-circuit of the little pond and came to the inlet, a brook with a barely discernable current about the

155

width of a bowling alley. Berry-laden bushes overhung it, forming a cool shaded tunnel. Their leaves had already turned crimson. Harbingers of autumn.

"Want an ex-plore?" I said to Mike. I had never ventured into that tunnel.

He shrugged again. Why not?

I pushed up through the archway of red-leaved bushes. We spooked a family of wood ducks. A hundred yards later the tunnel opened into a lazy creek. Although I knew we were in the middle of suburbia, we heard no traffic noises, saw no houses. It could have been wilderness. A muskrat swam across our bow. A kingfisher clattered away.

"Pretty, huh?" I said.

Mike nodded. At least it wasn't a shrug.

"Why don't you try to catch something?"

The shrug again. He began casting.

We paddled as far as we could. The creek narrowed and finally became impassable. We turned and moved back downstream. Mike made a few random casts. He had no hits. I sensed he'd rather have been playing ball with his friends.

As we approached the narrow tunnel that led to the pond, his rod suddenly bowed. "Got one," he said. Then, "Hey, I got a big one!"

Bluegill, I thought first. They can turn their sides to you and feel heavy. But the fish did not swim in characteristic bluegill circles. Bass, then. Maybe a pickerel.

Then it jumped near the bushes. The spinner flashed in the corner of its mouth. "It's a trout," I said. Then, louder, "Hey! You got a trout!"

Mike, an indifferent fisherman, nevertheless knew that trout were special. I saw his brow furrow. "What should I do?" he said through gritted teeth.

"You're doing fine. Don't rush it."

He did fine. The rainbow measured thirteen inches. I snapped Mike's picture holding it before he released it. He was smiling. No trace of a shrug.

I lied.

It happened ten years ago. Mike's a college man now.

But the rest of it's true, and it seems like it happened last week. I remember everything about that day. I have the picture, and the grin on my little boy's face reminds me of the time that an unlikely trout dissolved his shrug and hooked him on fishing.

There's also a brief notation in my tattered old fishing log:

Warner's Pond with Mike. Hot, muggy, no breeze. His first trout up in brook. Rainbow, thirteen inches on Mepps. Released. A few bluegills. Saw wood ducks.

I suppose even without the photo and the journal I wouldn't forget that day. With my memory joggers, however, it all comes washing over me. I like to sit back and savor the recollections, and I feel richer for it.

No excursion, however uneventful—or even disastrous—goes unrecorded. I go nowhere without my camera. Making my nightly entry into my log is as much a part of the post-trip ritual as stowing the rods and hanging the waders. Distilling the day's experiences into a few terse words sticks a satisfying period onto the end of each adventure. And now that record, both written and pictorial, goes back a couple decades. It helps me to recall it all. I can see the caddis swarming over the Bighorn, feel the throb in my wrist of one monster Frying Pan trout, smell the campfire deep in the Idaho canyons on the banks of the Middle Fork, hear the *Glug!* of a bass inhaling my deer-hair bug.

And I can see the grin of a boy transformed into an angler.

One wall of my writing room is hung heavy with framed photographs, each a memory jogger. A close-up of the twenty-four-
inch brown Andy nailed on the Bow River, with a monstrosity
he calls "The Fly That Ate Montana" tucked in the corner of
its mouth. Me in a float tube drifting ghostlike on the fuzzy
surface of Hebgen Lake the day the smoke from the Yellowstone
fire hung so thick over the water that the *Callibaetis* hatched
and the gulpers gulped all day. The five-pound largemouth that
took my bug the very first morning I fished with Andy. My first
Belize bonefish. A pastoral scene of the Paradise Valley. A
riverside lunch on the Missouri. My daughter, Melissa, holding
up a silvery flat-sided fish the day she proclaimed herself a
"crappie fisherman." The bluefish I took on a fly . . .

Sometimes I stand by my wall and surrender myself to the
memories. They last a long time. They keep me going until the
next trip. I still love to dwell upon what awaits me, the plans
I've made and those yet to be made. I find that looking backward makes the looking forward even more delicious. The older
I get, the more time I spend gazing upon my wall.

My journals have become more detailed in recent years. I
find I am increasingly fascinated by such things as weather and
fly hatches as well as angling success. I record the flies that
work and those that don't, and I sketch the designs for flies I
ought to invent at my tying table in the winter. Whatever I
notice, whatever ideas occur to me, I write them down. I like
to accumulate data and perform mathematical operations with
the variables. I never know what factor will prove to be significant. Water temperature, barometric pressure, time of day,
phase of moon. The places I go, the miles I drive, the money I
spend. The songs I whistle while fly-casting (usually Beatles
tunes, although I did awfully well one afternoon on Armstrong

Spring Creek with the second movement of Beethoven's Ninth—the music, as I recall, became monotonous, but the fishing didn't, so I stuck with Beethoven).

So far, I have concluded that randomness is easily the most significant variable in fishing success, but I'm still working on it. I'm also working on new definitions of success.

I do know that trout bite better when I leave my landing net in the car, and the dirty canvas hat with the Crazy Charlie bonefish fly impaled in the band works best.

My journals have become scrapbooks, bulging joggers for my increasingly fallible middle-aged memory. I keep track of everything I care about—the first robin and mating woodcock I see in the spring, the date of ice-out on New Hampshire's Lake Winnipesaukee, the first hatch of hendricksons on the Farmington. I paste in newspaper clippings. Here's one from a couple years ago explaining the new regulations on striped bass. Another, the obituary of an old fishing companion. A third details the sad plight of some of my beloved western rivers during the drought of 1988.

Here and there I've pasted in fading photographs. Many of them have come unstuck and fall out when I pick up the journal. It's fun to flip through it to find the place where the photos belong. A raggedy nymph under Scotch tape reminds me of the Bighorn brown trout that ate it. There's a letter from Peter Chenier reporting on the fabulous fishing his clients had on the Bow the week after Andy and I were there, and another from a ten-year-old girl in New Jersey who took up fishing after reading an article I wrote.

Last week my eight-year-old daughter Sarah caught her first trout. It was a cutthroat of about seven inches. It gobbled a

Blond Humpy that she had slopped out about fifteen feet into the Middle Fork of the Salmon River during the first fly-casting lesson of her life.

This time I'm telling the truth. It *was* last week, and I still see it sharply. She's perched barefoot on a boulder. Her brown eyes are round, her grin is wide, and her hair is snarled from two nights of sleeping in a tent. The rod is eight feet long, twice her size. The trout dangling from the leader she is holding up is a small flipping blur. In the background flows the river, and beyond it looms the canyon wall where, an hour earlier, we had spotted a pair of sheep.

The photo I'm looking at assures me that it will still seem like last week when I look at it again ten years from now.